Betty Crocker's
Chinese Cookbook

Random House, Inc. New York

FOREWORD

Welcome to the exciting discoveries of Chinese cooking. With the recipes in this book, new and exotic ingredients and the techniques of steaming, stir-frying and deep-frying, you can create delicious dishes to bring the pleasures of authentic Chinese dining into your own home.

Cantonese restaurant food long has been popular with Americans; and today, interest is growing in the spicier, more highly seasoned cooking of the Szechwan and Mandarin provinces of Northern China. In these pages, you will find recipes typical of all three cuisines.

Leeann Chin, who created these recipes, has authoritative, life-long knowledge of all these styles of Chinese cooking. Born in Canton, China, the daughter of Mandarin and Cantonese parents, Leeann became knowledgeable through inheritance and experience. At eighteen, she went to Hong Kong, where she married and later came with her husband and children to live in the United States. Today, she is widely known as cook, teacher of authentic Chinese cooking and proprietor of a beautiful, new contemporary restaurant, *Leeann Chin Chinese Cuisine,* in suburban Minneapolis, Minnesota.

Both in her restaurant and recipes, Leeann practices what she preaches — authentic Chinese cooking with imaginative innovations adapted to American tastes and ways. All of her recipes have been tested in the Betty Crocker Kitchens for success and practicality in kitchens just like yours. They are written in clear, easy-to-understand language and describe each step in the order in which it occurs. Ingredients and utensils are fully described and illustrated by photographs.

We recommend that you begin by preparing one or two dishes and introduce them into your meals. When you have mastered them, you will be ready to treat your family or guests to a simple all-Chinese meal, complete with rice and tea. You will find that Chinese food blends well with American dishes on the same menu, and that it is ideal for the casual entertaining we enjoy in the United States.

Consult the suggested menus in this book, then combine your own favorite dishes in menus of your own choosing. You will find Chinese cooking a fascinating hobby that all the family will want to share.

The Betty Crocker Editors

Copyright © 1981 by General Mills, Inc., Minneapolis, Minnesota

All rights reserved under International and Pan-American Copyright Conventions. Published in the United States by Random House, Inc., New York and simultaneously in Canada by Random House of Canada Limited, Toronto.

Library of Congress Cataloging in Publication Data   Recipes by Chin, Leeann, Betty Crocker's Chinese Cookbook.

Includes index.   1. Cookery, Chinese.   I. Crocker, Betty, pseud.   II. Title.   III. Title: Chinese Cookbook
TX724.5.C5C56115   641.5951   80-6044   ISBN 0-394-51881-0

Manufactured in the United States of America   3456789

CONTENTS

INTRODUCTION TO CHINESE COOKING

Chinese cooking is very appropriate to today's American lifestyle. It had its origins in ancient China where the cost of living was high and fuel and energy were scarce, just as they are now in the United States. The characteristic ingredients of Chinese dishes — lean meat, poultry and fish, crisp vegetables and rice — match our growing taste for lighter yet nutritious foods.

Centuries ago, when famine was a constant threat to the Chinese, rice became the mainstay of every meal because it was plentiful, filling and cheap. Meat and vegetables, which were more difficult to obtain, were eaten sparingly with the rice. As a symbol of security from hunger, therefore, rice came to be revered and cherished. The Chinese expression meaning "to eat dinner" is "sik fan," literally "to eat rice." And today, rice is still the main substance of a Chinese meal.

Early Chinese families cooked on small, portable, wood-burning stoves, which produced a high, intense flame on which food had to be cooked very quickly. Consequently, many ingredients in Chinese dishes are cut in small pieces or are thinly sliced to speed heat circulation and cooking time.

It is an adventure to experiment with exotic ingredients and unfamiliar utensils like the wok, skimmer and steamers. However, it is not really complicated. The ingredients listed here are available in supermarkets or in Chinese specialty food shops in most cities. And skillets, Dutch ovens and other standard American kitchen tools are adequate substitutes for the traditional Chinese utensils.

STIR-FRYING

Stir-frying is a Chinese method of cooking food quickly in a small amount of oil over high heat. When meat and vegetables are quickly tossed in hot oil, the meat remains tender and juicy and the vegetables crisp.

It is important to measure and prepare all ingredients before beginning to stir-fry. Just read the recipe completely before beginning. Assemble ingredients on a tray in the order in which they will be used. Place serving dishes near the range so that stir-fried food can be served immediately.

Always begin with a clean, dry wok. Before adding oil, heat the wok over high heat until a few drops of water sprinkled in it sizzle and evaporate. You then have what is called a "steaming hot wok." Use only 2 or 3 drops of water to test temperature; any remaining water in the wok will cause oil to splatter when it is added. If food sticks to the wok or moisture seeps from the meat and vegetables, the wok either is not sufficiently hot or too much food is being cooked at one time. If any food should stick, wash and dry the wok between steps as you cook.

Vegetable and peanut oil are used for stir-frying because they tolerate high heat. Margarine and butter are not used because they burn easily.

Use a spatula with a firm base, bringing it down the side of the wok and across the bottom to turn food over. Stir quickly; keeping food moving.

Stir-fried food is done when it changes in color; thinly sliced pork and chicken turn white and beef is no longer red. Vegetables become brighter in color while remaining crisp.

DEEP-FRYING

Deep-frying is a Chinese cooking method for foods dipped in batters. Ingredients are often marinated before deep-frying to develop their flavor. The actual frying is done in two stages rather than all at one time. First, the food is fried until light golden brown, then removed from the hot oil. In the second step, it is returned to the oil and fried until golden brown or done. This two-step method produces crisper texture and prevents food from overcooking on the outside before the inside is done. Deep-fried foods should be removed immediately from the oil and drained thoroughly.

A wok is especially suitable for deep-frying because, with its rounded bottom, it requires less oil. However, a deep, heavy saucepan or skillet or a Dutch oven will produce good results.

To deep-fry, pour in the required amount of oil. Heat uncovered since covering the wok during heating can cause the oil to overheat. Should this occur, turn off the heat and allow the oil to cool before proceeding.

With a deep fat thermometer, check the temperature of the oil at intervals during cooking. The temperature of the oil is critical. If it is too high, food will brown on the outside while the inside remains undone. Also, overheating oil causes it to deteriorate. On the other hand, if the oil is not sufficiently hot, food will sink to the bottom and will not surface immediately, resulting in soggy, greasy food.

With a fine wire strainer, remove cooked pieces of batter or food from the oil between steps in frying. Allow oil to return to recommended temperature before continuing to fry food.

If you wish to reuse oil for deep-frying, you must clarify and store it properly. To remove traces of fish flavor from oil that has been used for frying seafood, cook three to four slices of ginger in it until dark brown. Remove and discard the ginger. Allow oil to cool. Line a wire strainer with several layers of cheesecloth or paper towels. Place strainer in a bowl; pour the cooled oil into it. Store tightly covered in a clean bottle in the refrigerator.

STEAMING

Steaming is a Chinese cooking method used for meats, fish and dumplings. Steam uncooked foods in a single layer; reheat foods by steaming in several layers. To steam, cover food in bamboo steamer and place in wok. Carefully pour boiling water into the wok to a level of ½ inch below the bottom of the steamer. This amount of water will produce steam over high heat for about 25 minutes. If you find it necessary to add water, pour it down the inner side of the wok.

A metal or wooden rack placed in a wok, Dutch oven or electric skillet can be substituted for a bamboo steamer. Place food on a heatproof plate or bowl on the rack; cover with a tight-fitting lid which allows 1 to 2 inches of space above the food so that steam can circulate.

To improvise a steamer or rack, place empty cans, inverted heatproof bowls or chopsticks in the bottom of the wok or substitute pan. Place food on heatproof plate or bowl on top. Fill wok with boiling water to ½ inch of top of cans or bowl; cover tightly. Check water level during steaming; add more boiling water if necessary.

BLANCHING

Blanching is quick, partial cooking to preserve the texture, color and flavor of vegetables. To blanch, prepare vegetables according to the recipe. Place in a wire strainer and lower into boiling water; cover. Blanch tender vegetables like pea pods and green beans about 30 seconds or just until water returns to a boil. Blanch tougher vegetables like broccoli stems about two minutes. Rinse vegetables under running cold water or immediately plunge them into cold water to cool. Remove from water; drain. Vegetables are now ready to be used in the recipe.

UTENSILS

1. Chopsticks: In the Chinese language, the word "chopsticks" means "quick little ones." Chopsticks are used not only for eating, but also for beating eggs and stirring ingredients during cooking. Plastic, lacquered or ivory chopsticks are used for eating; bamboo or wooden ones are used for cooking and deep-frying since they do not bend or melt from heat. Chinese chopsticks differ in shape from the Japanese kind. They are longer, less tapered and have blunt tips for picking up food.

2. Spatula and Ladle: The spatula has a slightly curved edge to fit the shape of the wok and a slight lip to hold sauces. The ladle is shallow and bowl-shaped. Both utensils are of metal with long bamboo or wooden handles. Both utensils can be used to remove food from the wok to serving dishes. A pancake turner can be substituted for the spatula and a large spoon for the ladle.

3. Wire Ladle & Strainers: A wire mesh scoop with a flat bamboo or wooden handle is used for removing food from broth or oil. A fine mesh strainer is used to remove tiny bits of food which would otherwise remain in the oil to burn during deep-frying.

4. Wooden or Bamboo Tongs: Tongs are used for removing larger pieces of food from broth or oil.

5. Cleaver: This utensil has a sharp metal blade three to four inches broad and eight inches long. The large, heavy cleaver, called a "bone knife," is used to chop meat which includes bone. A thinner cleaver, lighter in weight, is used to slice meat and cut vegetables. Cleavers made of carbon steel are easily sharpened with a sharpening stone. However, they must be washed and dried by hand immediately after each use to prevent the blades from rusting and staining and the wooden handles from being damaged.

6. Steamers: Traditional Chinese steamers are round baskets made of bamboo with woven bottoms and lid. Steamers are used singly or stacked for steaming food in a wok containing boiling water. Steamers vary in size from four inches in diameter for cooking dim sum to 16 inches in diameter for seafood and poultry. The most versatile size is 10 inches in diameter. A metal or wooden rack placed in the wok can be substituted for the steamer. A heatproof plate containing food to be steamed is then placed on the rack.

7. Wok: This round-bottomed Chinese cooking vessel was designed for stir-frying in order to shorten cooking time and save fuel. The wok is nearly an all-purpose cooking utensil, which can be used to deep-dry, stir-fry, steam or stew food. While woks are made in sizes from 10 to 20 inches in diameter, the most versatile is 14 or 16 inches in diameter. The metal ringstand is to hold the round-bottomed wok securely on the surface of the range during cooking and can be used for safety.

The traditional bowl-shaped Chinese wok is made from heavy-gauge rolled carbon steel, which heats quickly and conducts heat evenly. However, woks made of carbon steel require some special care and thorough drying after each use to prevent rusting. To season a new wok, wash with hot sudsy water; dry on the range over medium heat. Rub about 2 teaspoons of vegetable oil evenly over the inside of the wok with a soft cloth. Repeat the process if food begins to stick.

Aluminum and stainless steel woks do not conduct heat as evenly as carbon steel. However, since they do not rust, they are a good choice for steaming foods. They require no seasoning and are easier to care for.

Electric woks, some with nonstick cooking surfaces, are convenient for cooking at the table. Follow manufacturer's directions for their care and use.

INGREDIENTS

1. Abalone: A mollusk with a flattened iridescent shell and smooth-textured meat. Avoid overcooking, which makes abalone tough and rubbery. Available fresh, canned or dried.

2. Baby Corn: Light yellow, miniature ears of corn, 1½ to 2 inches long. Tender and juicy. Sold canned in water.

3. Bamboo Shoots: Young, tender, ivory-colored shoots from the tropical bamboo plant. Used as a vegetable. Sold whole, sliced or in chunks, water-packed in cans. The tender, pointed end of the shoot is used for stir-frying; and the wide, less tender end is used for soups and stews or can be sliced very thin for stir-frying. Refrigerate bamboo shoots covered with cold water in a tightly-covered jar. Change the water daily.

4. Bean Curd: (Bean cakes). Bland, smooth, custard-like mixture made from puréed soybeans. Fragile and requires very little cooking. Used as an inexpensive vegetable and a good source of protein. Refrigerate bean curd covered with water and tightly covered. Change water daily.

5. Bean Sprouts: Young, white sprouts of the mung bean, which have a crisp texture and delicate flavor. Sold fresh or canned. Should be rinsed in cold water to retain their crispness. Refrigerate covered with cold water in a covered container; use within four days.

6. Black Beans, Salted: (Black fermented beans). Small, black, fermented soybeans; strong, pungent and salty in flavor. Sold in jars, cans or plastic bags of various sizes. Soak beans in warm water for 15 minutes; rinse to remove salt and skins. (Although the skins do not affect the flavor of the beans, they make the finished dish less attractive.) Refrigerate tightly covered after opening. Brown bean sauce can be substituted.

7. Bok Choy: (Chinese chard or white mustard cabbage). Resembles both chard and cabbage with crisp, white stalks and shiny, dark green leaves. Used cooked as a vegetable, in soups or in stir-fried dishes. Leaves can be separated from stalks and should be added to dishes last to prevent overcooking. Sold by the pound.

8. Brown Bean Sauce: (Brown bean paste). A thick, salty sauce made from fermented yellow soybeans, flour and salt. Adds flavor to cooked meats or sauces. Sold whole or mashed in cans or jars. Whole beans should be mashed before using. Refrigerate tightly covered after opening. Dark soy sauce can be substituted.

9. Chili Paste: (Chili paste with garlic, chili sauce or Szechwan paste). A hot, spicy sauce made from soybeans, hot peppers, salt, oil and garlic. Used in Szechwan cooking or as a condiment. Imported from Hong Kong and Taiwan and sold in jars or bottles. Refrigerate tightly covered after opening.

10. Chinese Cabbage: (Napa, celery cabbage or sui choy). Solid, oblong heads of long, smooth stalks with pale green leaves.

11. Chinese Parsley: (Cilantro or fresh coriander). A strongly flavored, aromatic herb with broad, flat, serrated leaves. Used as a garnish for hot and cold dishes. There is no substitute.

12. Egg Roll Skins: Thin, soft square sheets of dough made from eggs, flour and water. Used for wrapping meat, shrimp or vegetables to be deep-fried. Sold frozen or refrigerated.

13. Five-spice Powder: (Five spices, five-flavored powder, five-fragrance spice powder or five-fragrance powder). A mixture of five ground spices used to flavor food. It is slightly sweet and pungent. Star anise, cinnamon and cloves are usually three of the five spices used. Sold in jars or plastic bags. Store tightly covered in a dry place at room temperature.

14. Gingerroot: Gnarled brown root about three inches long used as a basic seasoning for Chinese cooking. Refrigerate tightly wrapped gingerroot or freeze it whole, sliced or chopped. There is no acceptable substitute for fresh gingerroot in Chinese recipes.

15. Hoisin Sauce: (Hoisen, hoison, haisein or Peking sauce). A thick, sweet reddish-brown sauce usually made from soybeans, vinegar, chilies, spices and garlic. Used in cooking and as a table condiment. Refrigerate tightly after opening. There is no substitute.

16. Mushrooms, Dried Black: (Chinese dried mushrooms, dried Chinese mushrooms, black dried mushrooms, winter mushrooms). Brownish-black mushrooms with caps that vary in size from ½ to 2 inches in diameter. Must be soaked in water until tender and washed before using. Store tightly covered at room temperature.

15.

9.

21.

13.

20.

23.

8.

6.

27.

Hoisin
Sauce

Chili
Paste

Powdered
Five Spices

Sesame
Oil

Plum
Sauce

Brown
Sauce

Fermented
Black Beans

Light
Soy Sauce

Heavy
Soy Sauce

Dark
Soy Sauce

7.

32.

10.

5.

11.

22.

29.

14.

16.

4.

24.

33.

28.

2.

12.

3.

26.

1.

31.

17.

19.

25.

18.

30.

17. Mushrooms, Straw: (Grass mushrooms). Tender, tall mushrooms with long leaf-like caps. Sold canned or dried. Soak the dried mushrooms and wash many times in warm water before using. Refrigerate the canned mushrooms covered with water after opening.

18. Noodles, Cellophane: (Bean threads, shining noodles, transparent noodles or vermicelli). Hard, clear white noodles made from mung peas. They become translucent, soft and gelatinous when they absorb liquid, and puffy and crisp when deep-fried. Sold in cellophane packages.

19. Noodles, Egg: An alimentary pasta made of flour and eggs, available dried or frozen. Served pan-fried or in soups. Thin egg noodles or spaghetti can be substituted.

20. Oil: Vegetable, peanut or corn oil can be used for deep-frying, stir-frying and marinating foods. Peanut oil has a higher smoking point but is less economical than vegetable oil. Sesame oil, made from roasted white sesame seeds, has a nut-like flavor and is used sparingly for flavoring. Sesame oil purchased from Oriental specialty stores is preferred to the paler, mild sesame oil sold in supermarkets. Refrigerate after opening to prevent rancidity.

21. Oyster Sauce: A thick, brown sauce made from oysters, salt, water and starch. Used as an ingredient or as a table condiment. Refrigerate tightly covered after opening. Half the amount of dark soy sauce can be substituted for the oyster sauce in recipes.

22. Pea Pods: (Snow peas or Chinese peas). Tender, flat, green edible pea pods. Add crispness, color and a delicate flavor to Chinese dishes. Sold fresh or frozen.

23. Plum Sauce: A thick, piquant sauce made from plums, apricots, chilies, vinegar and spices. Used as a table condiment for duck and spareribs and as an ingredient in sauces for appetizers.

24. Rice: There are two principal varieties of rice, long-grain and short-grain. Long-grain rice is generally preferred because it absorbs more water and is firmer when cooked. It should be washed in cold water until the water is clear to remove excess starch. Store rice at room temperature.

25. Rice Sticks: (Long rice or rice-flour noodles). Thin, brittle white noodles made from rice powder. They must be softened in liquid before stir-frying. When deep-fried they become puffy and crisp and are used as a garnish. Sold in cellophane packages and stored at room temperature.

26. Spring Roll Skins: Paper-thin, translucent squares or rounds of dough, similar to egg roll skins. Sold frozen or refrigerated.

27. Soy Sauce: A salty brown sauce made from soybeans, wheat, yeast and salt. There are three specific types: light, dark and heavy. Light soy sauce, light in color and delicately flavored, is used in clear soups and in marinades. Dark soy is made from the same ingredients as light, with the addition of caramel for a richer, darker color. Both light and dark soy sauces can be used as table condiments. Heavy soy sauce is made with molasses and is thick and dark. It is used for color in dark sauces. Oriental imported soy sauces are preferred because they are made by a slow, natural process of fermentation and aging. Soy sauce is sold in bottles or cans and can be stored at room temperature.

28. Tiger Lily Buds: (Tiger lily stems, lily buds, golden needles, lily flowers or tiger lilies). Pale-gold dried lily buds, 2 to 3 inches long, with a delicate, musky flavor. Used as a vegetable or for flavoring. Must be soaked in water before using. Sold in plastic bags and stored at room temperature.

29. Water Chestnuts: Crisp, white, delicately flavored bulb of an Asian marsh plant. Used as a vegetable for stir-frying and in soups and cold dishes. Available canned or fresh. If fresh, they must be washed and peeled before using.

30. Water Chestnut Flour: Lumpy gray flour made from water chestnuts, used as a thickener or as an ingredient in light, crisp batter.

31. Wheat Starch: Wheat flour with gluten removed, used for dim sum. No substitute.

32. Winter Melon: A round, green melon with translucent white pulp and yellow seeds. Sold whole or in pieces by the pound.

33. Wonton Skins: Thin, soft 3½-inch squares of dough made from eggs, flour and water. They are filled with meat, vegetable or seafood mixtures to be deep-fried, boiled or steamed. The corners can be removed and the rounds used for dumplings. Sold frozen or refrigerated.

MENUS

Fried Dumplings and Fried Wontons

Hot and Sour Soup or Wonton Soup

Mou Shu Pork

Wings with Black Beans

Pan-fried Shrimp or Lemon Chicken

Egg Rolls and Skewered Beef

Roast Duck

Stir-fried Bean Sprouts
with Black Mushrooms

Sweet and Sour Fish (Whole)

Steamed Rolls

Paper-wrapped Chicken
and Pork Dumplings

Shrimp Subgum Wonton

Sweet and Sour Pork
or
Sweet and Sour Chicken

Chicken Fried Rice

Shrimp Toast and Crispy Chicken Wings

Egg Drop Soup

Lemon Chicken

Stir-fried Pork with Cabbage
(Szechwan Style)
or
Stir-fried Beef with Broccoli

Steamed Fish with Bean Sauce

White Rice

Crabmeat Puffs and Barbecued Ribs

Sam See Soup

Sweet and Sour Fish (Whole)

Boneless Chicken with Almond Sauce

Stir-fried Beef with Bok Choy
or
Stir-fried Pork with Straw Mushrooms

Egg Rolls, Fried Wontons
and Barbecued Ribs

Roast Duck

Stir-fried Beef with Pea Pods
or
Chicken Almond Ding

Sweet and Sour Pork

White Rice or Stir-fried Rice

Egg Rolls,
Fried Dumplings with Shrimp Toast

Pressed Duck

Chicken Almond Ding

Sweet and Sour Pork

White Rice

DESSERT SUGGESTION

A combination of chilled pineapple chunks, mandarin oranges, kumquats, lychee nuts, strawberries and melon pieces on crushed ice in a bowl.

Note: See additional menu suggestions on pages 25, 35, 73 and 81.

Appetizers

Chicken Wing Drumsticks

10 chicken wings
 1 tablespoon cornstarch
 1 teaspoon sugar
 1 teaspoon salt
 1 teaspoon light soy sauce
 ½ teaspoon five spice powder

 Vegetable oil
 ½ cup all-purpose flour
 ½ cup water
 1 egg
 3 tablespoons cornstarch
 2 tablespoons vegetable oil
 ½ teaspoon baking soda
 ½ teaspoon salt

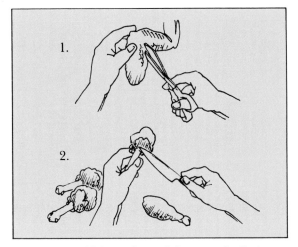

(1) Cut each chicken wing at joint to make 2 pieces; reserve piece with tip to use in Chicken Broth (page 26). (2) Cut skin and meat loose from narrow end of bone; push meat and skin down to large end of bone. Pull skin and meat down over end of bone to form a ball. Mix 1 tablespoon cornstarch, the sugar, 1 teaspoon salt, the soy sauce and five spice powder; sprinkle over chicken drumsticks. Cover and refrigerate 30 minutes.

Heat vegetable oil (1½ inches) in wok to 350°. Mix flour, water, egg, 3 tablespoons cornstarch, 2 tablespoons vegetable oil, the baking soda and ½ teaspoon salt. Dip ball end of each drumstick into batter. Fry 5 drumsticks at a time until light brown, turning 2 or 3 times, 4 to 5 minutes. Drain on paper towel. Increase oil temperature to 375°. Fry drumsticks all at one time until golden brown, about 2 minutes. Drain on paper towel. Serve with Hot Mustard and a sweet and sour sauce (pages 14 and 20) if desired. *10 drumsticks.*

Barbecued Ribs

2½ to 3-pound rack pork back ribs, cut lengthwise across bones into halves
 2 tablespoons sugar
 1 tablespoon salt
 2 large cloves garlic, finely chopped
 ½ cup catsup
 2 tablespoons Hoisin sauce
 1 tablespoon dry white wine

Trim fat and remove membranes from ribs; place ribs in shallow glass or plastic dish. Mix remaining ingredients. Pour mixture over ribs; turn ribs. Cover and refrigerate at least 2 hours.

Place ribs in single layer on rack in roasting pan; brush with sauce. Cook uncovered in 400° oven 30 minutes. Turn ribs; brush with sauce. Cook uncovered until done, about 30 minutes longer. (Reduce oven temperature to 375° if ribs are thin.) Cut between each rib to separate; serve with Hot Mustard (page 14) if desired. *35 to 40 appetizers.*

Do-ahead Directions: Prepare Barbecued Ribs; wrap, label and freeze no longer than 2 months. Just before serving, cover frozen ribs and heat in 350° oven 20 minutes. Uncover and heat until hot, about 20 minutes.

Top: Barbecued Ribs, Right: Red Sweet and Sour Sauce, Bottom: Chicken Wing Drumsticks, Left: Hot Mustard

Barbecued Pork

3   pound fresh pork blade Boston roast
2   tablespoons sugar
1   tablespoon salt
1   clove garlic, finely chopped
1/2 cup catsup
2   tablespoons Hoisin sauce
1   tablespoon dry sherry

Trim fat from pork; cut pork into 1-inch slices. Place in glass or plastic bowl. Mix remaining ingredients; pour over pork. Turn pork to coat with marinade. Cover and refrigerate at least 2 hours.

Place pork in single layer on rack in shallow roasting pan. Brush with half of the marinade. Cook uncovered in 400° oven 30 minutes. Turn pork; brush with remaining marinade. Cook uncovered until done, about 30 minutes. Cut into 1/4-inch slices; serve with Hot Mustard and a sweet and sour sauce (page 20) if desired. *40 to 50 appetizers.*

Do-ahead Directions: Prepare Barbecued Pork; wrap, label and freeze no longer than 2 months. Just before serving, cover frozen pork and heat in 350° oven 30 minutes. Uncover and heat until hot, about 20 minutes. Cut into 1/4-inch slices.

Red Sweet and Sour Sauce

1/2 cup red wine vinegar
1/2 cup catsup
1/3 cup sugar
15 drops red pepper sauce

Mix all ingredients; cover and refrigerate. Serve with appetizers. *1 1/4 cups.*

Crispy Fried Spareribs

2   pound rack pork back ribs, cut lengthwise across
        bones into halves
1   egg
2   tablespoons vegetable oil
2   teaspoons cornstarch
1   teaspoon salt
1   teaspoon soy sauce (light or dark)
1/2 teaspoon five spice powder

    Vegetable oil
3/4 cup all-purpose flour
2   tablespoons cornstarch
1   teaspoon salt
1/2 teaspoon baking soda

Trim fat and remove membranes from ribs. Cut between each rib to separate. Mix egg, 2 tablespoons vegetable oil, 2 teaspoons cornstarch, 1 teaspoon salt, the soy sauce and five spice powder in glass or plastic bowl; stir in ribs. Cover and refrigerate 30 minutes. Drain ribs; reserve marinade.

Heat vegetable oil (1 1/2 inches) in wok to 350°. Add enough water to reserved marinade to measure 3/4 cup. Mix marinade, flour, 2 tablespoons cornstarch, 1 teaspoon salt and the baking soda. Stir ribs into batter until well coated. Fry 10 to 12 ribs at a time until light brown, turning occasionally, 3 to 4 minutes. Drain on paper towel. Increase oil temperature to 375°. Fry ribs all at one time until golden brown, about 1 minute. Drain on paper towel. Serve with Hot Mustard and a sweet and sour sauce (page 20) if desired. *30 to 36 appetizers.*

Do-ahead Directions: After frying ribs 3 to 4 minutes, wrap, label and freeze no longer than 1 week. Heat frozen ribs uncovered in 425° oven until hot, 20 to 25 minutes. Drain on paper towel.

Hot Mustard

Stir 1/4 cup dry mustard and 3 tablespoons plus 1 1/2 teaspoons cold water until smooth. Let stand 5 minutes before serving. Cover and refrigerate any remaining mustard. *1/3 cup.*

Skewered Chicken

2   whole chicken breasts (about 2 pounds)
1   tablespoon vegetable oil
2   teaspoons dry white wine
1   teaspoon finely chopped gingerroot
1   teaspoon cornstarch
1   teaspoon salt
1   teaspoon dark soy sauce
1/2 teaspoon sugar
1/4 teaspoon white pepper
1/4 teaspoon sesame oil
1   medium onion

Remove bones and skin from chicken; cut chicken into strips, 2 × 1/2 inch. Toss chicken, vegetable oil, wine, gingerroot, cornstarch, salt, soy sauce, sugar, white pepper and sesame oil in glass or plastic bowl. Cover and refrigerate 30 minutes. Cut onion into 1-inch pieces.

Thread 1 onion piece, 2 chicken strips and 1 onion piece on each of thirty-six 6-inch skewers. Set oven control to broil and/or 550°. Broil with tops about 4 inches from heat, turning once, until done, about 5 minutes. *36 appetizers.*

Note: Soak wooden skewers in water before using.

Paper-wrapped Chicken

3   pound broiler-fryer chicken, cut up
1   tablespoon vegetable oil
2   teaspoons dry white wine
1   teaspoon cornstarch
1   teaspoon finely chopped gingerroot
1   teaspoon salt
1   teaspoon dark soy sauce
1/2 teaspoon sugar
1/4 teaspoon white pepper
1/4 teaspoon sesame oil

   Thirty 5-inch squares aluminum foil, parchment
      or waxed paper

   Vegetable oil

Remove bones and skin from chicken; cut chicken into strips, 2 × 1/2 inch. Toss chicken, 1 tablespoon vegetable oil, the wine, cornstarch, gingerroot, salt, soy sauce, sugar, white pepper and sesame oil in glass or plastic bowl. Cover and refrigerate 1 hour. Place 3 or 4 strips chicken slightly below center of foil square.

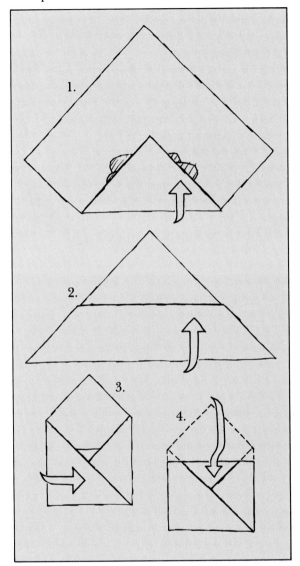

(1) Fold corner of square closest to chicken over chicken. (2) Fold up again. (3) Overlap the two opposite corners. (4) Fold fourth corner down and tuck under overlapped corners. Chicken must be securely sealed in foil. Repeat with remaining foil squares.

Heat oil (1½ inches) in wok to 350°. Fry 10 packets at a time, turning 3 or 4 times, about 3 minutes. Drain on paper towel. *30 appetizers.*

Crispy Chicken Wings

12	chicken wings
1	egg
2	teaspoons vegetable oil
2	teaspoons soy sauce (light or dark)
1	teaspoon salt
1	teaspoon sugar
1/2	teaspoon five spice powder
1/4	cup water
1/2	cup all-purpose flour
1/4	cup cornstarch
1/2	teaspoon baking soda
	Vegetable oil

Cut each chicken wing at joints to make 3 pieces; reserve tip to use in Chicken Broth (page 26). Mix egg, 2 teaspoons vegetable oil, the soy sauce, salt, sugar and five spice powder; pour over chicken. Cover and refrigerate 1 hour.

Add water to chicken. Stir flour, cornstarch and baking soda into chicken.

Heat vegetable oil (1½ inches) in wok to 350°. Fry 4 or 5 chicken pieces at a time until light brown, turning 2 or 3 times, about 4 minutes; drain on paper towel. Increase oil temperature to 375°. Fry half of the chicken pieces until golden brown, about 1 minute. Drain on paper towel. Repeat with remaining pieces. Serve with sweet and sour sauce or Hot Mustard (page 14) if desired. *6 servings.*

Skewered Beef

1	pound beef flank steak
2	tablespoons vegetable oil
2	teaspoons soy sauce (light or dark)
1	teaspoon finely chopped gingerroot
1	teaspoon sugar
1	teaspoon salt
1	teaspoon dry white wine
1/4	teaspoon white pepper
1	medium onion

Cut beef across grain into ⅛-inch strips. Toss beef, vegetable oil, soy sauce, gingerroot, sugar, salt, wine and white pepper in glass or plastic bowl. Cover and refrigerate 30 minutes. Cut onion into 1-inch pieces.

Thread 1 onion piece, 1 beef strip and 1 onion piece on each of thirty 6-inch skewers. Set oven control to broil and/or 550°. Broil with tops about 4 inches from heat, turning once, until done, about 6 minutes. *30 appetizers.*

Note: Soak wooden skewers in water before using.

Left to right: Crispy Chicken Wings, Skewered Beef, Crispy Fried Shrimp, Lemon Sauce

Crispy Fried Shrimp

1   pound fresh or frozen raw shrimp
1   egg, slightly beaten
1   tablespoon cornstarch
1   teaspoon dry white wine
½   teaspoon light soy sauce
¼   teaspoon salt

    Vegetable oil
½   cup all-purpose flour
½   cup water
3   tablespoons cornstarch
1   tablespoon vegetable oil
½   teaspoon baking soda
½   teaspoon salt

Remove shells from shrimp, leaving tails intact. (If shrimp is frozen, do not thaw; peel under running cold water.) Make a shallow cut lengthwise down back of each shrimp; wash out sand vein. Slit shrimp lengthwise down back almost in half. Mix egg, 1 tablespoon cornstarch, the wine, soy sauce and ¼ teaspoon salt in glass or plastic bowl; stir in shrimp. Cover and refrigerate 10 minutes.

Heat vegetable oil (1½ inches) in wok to 375°. Mix flour, water, 3 tablespoons cornstarch, 1 tablespoon vegetable oil, the baking soda and ½ tea-spoon salt. Stir shrimp into batter until well coated. Fry 5 or 6 shrimp at a time until golden brown, turning occasionally, 2 to 3 minutes. Drain on paper towel. Serve with Hot Mustard, a sweet and sour sauce (pages 14 and 20) and Lemon Sauce if desired. *About 20 shrimp.*

Lemon Sauce

¼   cup chicken broth or water
2   tablespoons lemon juice
2   tablespoons honey
1   tablespoon vinegar
1   tablespoon vegetable oil
1½ teaspoons catsup
¼   teaspoon garlic salt
1   teaspoon cornstarch
1   teaspoon cold water

Heat chicken broth, lemon juice, honey, vinegar, vegetable oil, catsup and garlic salt to boiling in 1-quart saucepan. Mix cornstarch and water; stir into broth mixture. Heat to boiling, stirring constantly. Cover and refrigerate. Serve with appetizers. *⅔ cup.*

Fried Chicken Wontons

1   *whole chicken breast (about 1 pound)*
3   *canned water chestnuts, finely chopped*
1/4 *cup chopped green onions (with tops)*
2   *teaspoons vegetable oil*
1   *teaspoon cornstarch*
1   *teaspoon salt*
1   *teaspoon light soy sauce*
    Dash of white pepper

1   *pound wonton skins*
1   *egg, slightly beaten*

    Vegetable oil

Remove bones and skin from chicken; finely chop chicken. Mix chicken, water chestnuts, green onions, 2 teaspoons vegetable oil, the cornstarch, salt, soy sauce and white pepper.

Place 1/2 teaspoon chicken mixture in center of wonton skin. (Cover remaining skins with dampened towel to keep them pliable.) Fold bottom corner of wonton skin over filling to opposite corner, forming a triangle. Brush right corner of triangle with egg. Bring corners together below filling; pinch left corner to right corner to seal. (See illustrations, page 27.) Repeat with remaining wonton skins. (Cover filled wontons with dampened towel or plastic wrap to keep them from drying out.)

Heat oil (1 1/2 inches) in wok to 350°. Fry 8 to 10 wontons at a time until golden brown, turning 2 or 3 times, about 3 minutes. Drain on paper towel. Serve with Hot Mustard and a sweet and sour sauce (pages 14 and 20) if desired. *50 to 60 appetizers.*

Do-ahead Directions: Prepare Fried Chicken Wontons; wrap, label and freeze no longer than 3 months. Just before serving, heat frozen wontons uncovered in 400° oven until hot, 10 to 12 minutes.

Fried Wontons

1/2 *pound fresh or frozen raw shrimp*
1/4 *pound ground pork*
6   *canned water chestnuts, finely chopped*
1/4 *cup chopped green onions (with tops)*
1   *teaspoon cornstarch*
1   *teaspoon salt*
1/8 *teaspoon sesame oil*
    Dash of white pepper

1   *pound wonton skins*
1   *egg, slightly beaten*

    Vegetable oil

Peel shrimp. (If shrimp is frozen, do not thaw; peel under running cold water.) Make a shallow cut lengthwise down back of each shrimp; wash out sand vein. Chop shrimp finely. Mix shrimp, pork, water chestnuts, green onions, cornstarch, salt, sesame oil and white pepper.

Place 1/2 teaspoon shrimp mixture in center of wonton skin. (Cover remaining skins with dampened towel to keep them pliable.) Fold bottom corner of wonton skin over filling to opposite corner, forming a triangle. Brush right corner of triangle with egg. Bring corners together below filling; pinch left corner to right corner to seal. (See illustrations on page 27.) Repeat with remaining wonton skins. (Cover wontons with dampened towel or plastic wrap to keep them from drying out.)

Heat oil (1 1/2 inches) in wok to 350°. Fry 8 to 10 wontons at a time until golden brown, turning 2 or 3 times, about 3 minutes. Drain on paper towel. Serve with Hot Mustard and a sweet and sour sauce (pages 14 and 20) if desired. *50 to 60 appetizers.*

Do-ahead Directons: Prepare Fried Wontons; wrap, label and freeze no longer than 1 month. Just before serving, heat frozen wontons uncovered in 400° oven until hot, 10 to 12 minutes.

Chicken Egg Rolls

8	to 10 dried black mushrooms
2	whole chicken breasts (about 2 pounds)
1	teaspoon salt
1	teaspoon cornstarch
2	pounds bean sprouts
3	tablespoons vegetable oil
2	teaspoons salt
2	teaspoons five spice powder
3	tablespoons vegetable oil
½	cup shredded canned bamboo shoots
½	cup sliced green onions (with tops)
1	pound egg roll skins
1	egg, beaten
	Vegetable oil

Soak mushrooms in warm water until soft, about 30 minutes; drain. Rinse in warm water; drain. Remove and discard stems; shred caps. Remove bones and skin from chicken; shred chicken (see page 52). Mix chicken, 1 teaspoon salt and the cornstarch. Rinse bean sprouts in cold water; drain.

Heat wok until 1 or 2 drops of water bubble and skitter when sprinkled in wok. Add 3 tablespoons vegetable oil; rotate wok to coat side. Add bean sprouts; stir-fry 2 minutes. Mix 2 teaspoons salt and the five spice powder; stir half of the mixture into bean sprouts. Remove bean sprouts from wok.

Add 3 tablespoons vegetable oil to wok; rotate to coat side. Add chicken; stir-fry until chicken turns white. Add mushrooms and bamboo shoots; stir-fry 2 minutes. Stir in bean sprouts, remaining five spice powder mixture and the green onions; drain thoroughly and cool.

Prepare egg roll as illustrated below. Repeat with remaining egg roll skins. (Cover filled egg rolls with dampened towel or plastic wrap to keep them from drying out.)

Heat vegetable oil (2 inches) in wok to 350°. Fry 4 or 5 egg rolls at a time until golden brown, turning 2 or 3 times, 2 to 3 minutes. Drain on paper towel. Serve with Hot Mustard and a sweet and sour sauce (pages 14 and 20) if desired. *18 to 22 egg rolls.*

Do-ahead Directions: Prepare Chicken Egg Rolls; wrap, label and freeze no longer than 3 months. Just before serving, place frozen rolls on rack in jelly roll pan, 15½ × 10½ × 1 inch. Heat uncovered in 425° oven until hot, about 30 minutes.

How to Make Egg Rolls

1. Place ½ cup mixture slightly below center of egg roll skin. Cover remaining skins with dampened towel to keep them pliable.

2. Fold corner of egg roll skin closest to filling over filling, tucking the points under.

3. Fold in and overlap the two opposite corners.

4. Brush fourth corner with egg; roll up enclosed filling to seal.

Egg Rolls

4   *or 5 medium dried black mushrooms*
1/2 *pound ground pork*
1/2 *teaspoon salt*
1/2 *teaspoon cornstarch*
1/2 *teaspoon soy sauce*
     Dash of white pepper

8   *cups water*
1   *head green cabbage (about 2 1/2 pounds),*
     finely shredded

2   *tablespoons vegetable oil*
1/4 *cup shredded canned bamboo shoots*
1/2 *pound cooked shrimp, finely chopped*
1/3 *cup finely chopped green onions (with tops)*
1   *teaspoon salt*
1   *teaspoon five spice powder*

1   *pound egg roll skins*
1   *egg, beaten*

     Vegetable oil

Soak mushrooms in warm water until soft, about 30 minutes; drain. Rinse in warm water; drain. Remove and discard stems; cut caps into thin strips. Mix pork, 1/2 teaspoon salt, the cornstarch, soy sauce and white pepper. Cover and refrigerate about 20 minutes.

Heat water to boiling in 4-quart Dutch oven; add cabbage. Heat to boiling; cover and cook 1 minute. Drain; rinse with cold water until cabbage is cold. Drain thoroughly; remove excess water by squeezing cabbage.

Heat wok until 1 or 2 drops of water bubble and skitter when sprinkled in wok. Add 2 tablespoons vegetable oil; rotate to coat side. Add pork; stir-fry until pork is no longer pink. Add mushrooms and bamboo shoots; stir-fry 1 minute. Stir in cabbage, shrimp, green onions, 1 teaspoon salt and the five spice powder; cool.

Place 1/2 cup pork mixture slightly below center of egg roll skin. (Cover remaining skins with damp-ened towel to keep them pliable.) Fold corner of egg roll skin closest to filling over filling, tucking the point under. Fold in and overlap the two oppo-site corners. Brush fourth corner with egg; roll up enclosed filling to seal. (See illustrations on page 19.) Repeat with remaining egg roll skins. (Cover filled egg rolls with dampened towel or plastic wrap to keep them from drying out.)

Heat vegetable oil (2 inches) in wok to 350°. Fry 4 or 5 egg rolls at a time until golden brown, turning 2 or 3 times, 2 to 3 minutes. Drain on paper towel. Serve with Hot Mustard and a sweet and sour sauce (page 14) if desired. *16 to 18 egg rolls.*

Plum Sweet and Sour Sauce

1   *can (20 ounces) crushed pineapple in heavy syrup*
1   *cup sugar*
1   *cup water*
1   *cup vinegar*
1   *tablespoon dark soy sauce*
2   *tablespoons cornstarch*
2   *tablespoons cold water*
1   *cup plum sauce or plum jam**

*Orange marmalade can be substituted for the plum sauce.

Heat pineapple (with syrup), sugar, 1 cup water, the vinegar and soy sauce to boiling. Mix corn-starch and 2 tablespoons water; stir into pineapple mixture. Heat to boiling, stirring constantly. Cool to room temperature; stir in plum sauce. Cover and refrigerate. Serve with appetizers. *5 2/3 cups.*

Egg Rolls and Plum Sweet and Sour Sauce

Spring Rolls

8   or 10 dried black mushrooms
2   pounds bean sprouts
1   cup cooked shrimp

1/4   cup vegetable oil
1/2   cup shredded canned bamboo shoots
2   teaspoons salt
2   teaspoons five spice powder
1   cup shredded Barbecued Pork (page 14)
1/2   cup finely chopped green onions (with tops)

1   pound spring roll skins
1   egg, slightly beaten

   Vegetable oil

Soak mushrooms in warm water until soft, about 30 minutes; drain. Rinse in warm water; drain. Remove and discard stems; shred caps. Rinse bean sprouts in cold water; drain. Cut shrimp into ½-inch pieces.

Heat wok until 2 drops of water bubble and skitter when sprinkled in wok. Add ¼ cup vegetable oil; rotate wok. Add bean sprouts; stir-fry 1 minute. Add mushrooms, bamboo shoots, salt and five spice powder; stir-fry 2 minutes. Remove vegetables from wok; drain and cool. Stir shrimp, Barbecued Pork and green onions into vegetables.

Place ⅓ cup Barbecued Pork mixture slightly below center of spring roll skin. (Cover remaining skins with dampened towel to keep them pliable.) Fold corner of spring roll skin closest to filling over filling, tucking the point under. Fold in and overlap the two opposite corners. Brush fourth corner with egg; roll up enclosed filling to seal. (See illustrations on page 19.) Repeat with remaining spring roll skins. (Cover spring rolls with dampened towel or plastic wrap to keep them from drying out.)

Heat vegetable oil (2 inches) in wok to 350°. Fry 4 or 5 rolls at a time until golden brown, turning 2 or 3 times, about 3 minutes. Drain on paper towel. Serve with Hot Mustard and a sweet and sour sauce (pages 14 and 20) if desired. *20 to 25 spring rolls.*

Do-ahead Directions: Prepare Spring Rolls; wrap, label and freeze no longer than 3 months. Just before serving, place frozen rolls on rack in jelly roll pan, 15½ × 10½ × 1 inch. Heat uncovered in 425° oven until hot, about 25 minutes.

Crabmeat Puffs

1   package (6 ounces) frozen crabmeat, drained
      and cartilage removed, chopped
2   packages (3 ounces each) cream cheese, softened
1/2   teaspoon salt
1/4   teaspoon garlic powder

40   wonton skins
1   egg, slightly beaten

   Vegetable oil

Mix chopped crabmeat, cream cheese, salt and garlic powder.

Brush wonton skin with egg.

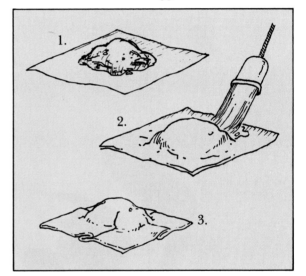

(1) Place heaping teaspoonful crabmeat mixture in center of wonton skin. (Cover remaining skins with dampened towel to keep them pliable.) (2) Top with another wonton skin; press edges to seal. Brush dab of egg on center of each side of puff. (3) Make a pleat on each edge, pressing to seal. Repeat with remaining wonton skins. (Cover puffs with dampened towel or plastic wrap to keep them from drying out.)

Heat vegetable oil (1½ inches) in wok to 350°. Fry 4 or 5 puffs at a time until golden brown, turning 2 or 3 times, about 2 minutes. Drain on paper towel. Serve with Lemon Sauce (page 17) if desired. *20 appetizers.*

Do-ahead Directions: Prepare Crabmeat Puffs; wrap, label and freeze no longer than 6 weeks. Just before serving, heat frozen puffs uncovered in 400° oven until hot, about 10 minutes. Drain on paper towel.

Shrimp Toast

½ pound fresh or frozen raw shrimp
½ cup chopped green onions (with tops)
¼ cup all-purpose flour
¼ cup water
1 egg
1 tablespoon cornstarch
1 teaspoon salt
¼ teaspoon sugar
¼ teaspoon sesame oil
   Dash of white pepper

   Vegetable oil
5 slices white bread

Peel shrimp. (If shrimp is frozen, do not thaw; peel under running cold water.) Make a shallow cut lengthwise down back of each shrimp; wash out sand vein. Cut shrimp lengthwise into halves; cut crosswise into halves.

Mix shrimp, green onions, flour, water, egg, cornstarch, salt, sugar, sesame oil and white pepper.

Heat vegetable oil (1½ inches) in wok to 350°. Remove crusts from bread; cut each slice into 4 squares. Place 1 or 2 pieces shrimp with sauce on each bread square.

Fry 5 squares at a time until golden brown, turning frequently, about 2 minutes. Drain on paper towel. *20 appetizers.*

Do-ahead Directions: Prepare Shrimp Toast; cover and refrigerate no longer than 24 hours. Just before serving, heat uncovered in 400° oven until hot, 12 to 15 minutes. Drain on paper towel.

Fish Toast

1 cup water
2 strips bacon, finely chopped
½ pound walleye or sea bass fillets
4 canned water chestnuts, finely chopped
¼ cup water
1 large green onion (with top), finely chopped
2 tablespoons all-purpose flour
1 teaspoon cornstarch
1 teaspoon salt
¼ teaspoon finely chopped gingerroot
¼ teaspoon white pepper
¼ teaspoon sesame oil

   Vegetable oil
7 slices white bread

Heat 1 cup water to boiling. Add bacon; heat to boiling. Cover and boil 2 minutes; drain. Remove skin from fish; chop fish finely. Mix bacon, fish, water chestnuts, ¼ cup water, the green onion, flour, cornstarch, salt, gingerroot, white pepper and sesame oil.

Heat vegetable oil (1½ inches) in wok to 350°. Remove crusts from bread; cut each slice into 4 squares. Spread 1 teaspoon fish mixture over each bread square. Fry 7 squares at a time until golden brown, turning frequently, about 2½ minutes. Drain·on paper towel. *28 appetizers.*

Do-ahead Directons: Prepare Fish Toast; cover and refrigerate no longer than 24 hours. Just before serving, heat uncovered in 400° oven until hot, 10 to 12 minutes. Drain on paper towel.

Soups

Winter Melon Soup

6   medium dried black mushrooms
1   whole chicken breast (about 1 pound)
½   teaspoon cornstarch
½   teaspoon salt
1   pound winter melon
4   ounces fully cooked smoked ham
½   cup sliced canned bamboo shoots

4   cups chicken broth
1   teaspoon salt
⅛   teaspoon white pepper

Soak mushrooms in warm water until soft; drain. Rinse in warm water; drain. Remove and discard stems; cut caps into ¼-inch pieces.

Remove bones and skin from chicken; cut chicken into ½-inch pieces. Toss chicken, cornstarch and ½ teaspoon salt in glass or plastic bowl. Cover and refrigerate 20 minutes.

Remove rind, seeds and fibers from winter melon; cut melon into ½-inch pieces. Cut ham and bamboo shoots into ½-inch pieces.

Heat chicken broth to boiling in 3-quart saucepan. Add mushrooms, melon and bamboo shoots; heat to boiling. Stir in chicken and ham. Heat to boiling; reduce heat. Cover and simmer 10 minutes. Stir in 1 teaspoon salt and the white pepper. *6 servings (about 1 cup each).*

Bean Curd Soup

6   medium dried black mushrooms
12 ounces bean curd
4   ounces pea pods

4   cups chicken broth
1   teaspoon salt

Soak mushrooms in warm water until soft, about 30 minutes; drain. Rinse in warm water; drain. Remove and discard stems; cut each cap into 4 pieces. Cut bean curd into ¾-inch squares. Remove strings from pea pods.

Heat chicken broth to boiling in 3-quart saucepan. Stir in mushrooms, bean curd and salt. Heat to boiling; reduce heat. Cover and simmer 5 minutes. Add pea pods; heat just to boiling. *6 servings (about 1 cup each).*

MENU

Crabmeat Puffs and Pork Dumplings

Winter Melon Soup

Stuffed Shrimp

Mandarin Beef

Steamed Fish with Bean Sauce

Winter Melon Soup

Chicken and Spinach Soup

1   whole chicken breast (about 1 pound)
½   teaspoon cornstarch
½   teaspoon salt
    Dash of pepper
8   ounces spinach

4   cups chicken broth
3   thin slices gingerroot
1   teaspoon salt
⅛   teaspoon white pepper

Remove bones and skin from chicken; shred chicken (see page 52). Toss chicken, cornstarch, ½ teaspoon salt and dash of pepper. Tear spinach into bite-size pieces.

Heat chicken broth and gingerroot to boiling in 3-quart saucepan. Stir in chicken; heat to boiling.

Stir in spinach, 1 teaspoon salt and the white pepper. Heat to boiling; reduce heat. Cover and simmer until spinach is tender, about 2 minutes. Remove gingerroot. *6 servings (about 1 cup each).*

Chicken Broth

Cover giblets, bones from boned chicken and 2 slices gingerroot with boiling water. Heat to boiling; reduce heat. Cover and simmer 1½ to 2 hours. Strain broth; serve immediately or reserve to use in cooking (see below).

Do-ahead Directions: Cover and refrigerate broth no longer than 4 days or freeze no longer than 6 months. Dip frozen container into hot water just to loosen. Place frozen block in saucepan. Cover tightly; heat, stirring occasionally, until thawed.

Beef with Vegetable Soup

½   pound beef flank or boneless sirloin steak
½   teaspoon chopped gingerroot
½   teaspoon cornstarch
½   teaspoon salt
½   teaspoon soy sauce (light or dark)
½   teaspoon vegetable oil
    Dash of white pepper
3   large stalks bok choy or celery cabbage

4   cups chicken broth or beef broth
1   teaspoon salt

Trim fat from beef; cut beef with grain into 2-inch strips. Cut strips across grain into ⅛-inch slices. Toss beef, gingerroot, cornstarch, ½ teaspoon salt, the soy sauce, vegetable oil and white pepper in glass or plastic bowl. Cover and refrigerate 20 minutes. Cut bok choy (with leaves) into pieces, 2 × ½ inch.

Heat chicken broth to boiling in 3-quart saucepan. Add bok choy and 1 teaspoon salt; heat to boiling. Boil uncovered 2 minutes. Stir in beef; heat to boiling. Boil uncovered 1 minute. *6 servings (about 1 cup each).*

Egg Drop Soup

3   cups chicken broth
1   teaspoon salt
    Dash of white pepper
1   medium green onion (with top), chopped
2   eggs, slightly beaten

Heat chicken broth, salt and white pepper to boiling in 2-quart saucepan. Stir green onion into eggs. Pour egg mixture slowly into broth, stirring constantly with fork until egg forms shreds. *3 servings (about 1 cup each).*

Wonton Soup

¼   pound fresh or frozen raw shrimp
2   ounces ground pork
3   canned water chestnuts, finely chopped
2   green onions (with tops), chopped
1   teaspoon cornstarch
½   teaspoon salt
¼   teaspoon sesame oil
      Dash of white pepper

24   wonton skins
1   egg white, slightly beaten
5   cups water

½   chicken breast (about ½ pound)
½   teaspoon cornstarch
½   teaspoon salt
      Dash of white pepper
4   ounces pea pods
4   ounces mushrooms

4   cups chicken broth
¼   cup sliced canned bamboo shoots
1   teaspoon salt
      Dash of white pepper
2   tablespoons chopped green onions (with tops)
¼   teaspoon sesame oil

Peel shrimp. (If shrimp is frozen, do not thaw; peel under running cold water.) Make a shallow cut lengthwise down back of each shrimp; wash out sand vein. Chop shrimp finely. Mix shrimp, pork, water chestnuts, 2 green onions, 1 teaspoon cornstarch, ½ teaspoon salt, ¼ teaspoon sesame oil and dash of white pepper.

(1) Place ½ teaspoon shrimp mixture in center of wonton skin. (Cover remaining skins with dampened towel to keep them pliable.) (2) Fold bottom corner of wonton skin over filling to opposite corner, forming a triangle. Brush right corner of triangle with egg white. (3) Bring corners together below filling; pinch left corner to right corner to seal. Repeat with remaining wonton skins. (Cover filled wontons with dampened towel to keep them from drying out.) Heat water to boiling in 4-quart Dutch oven; add wontons. Heat to boiling; reduce heat. Simmer uncovered 2 minutes; drain. Rinse wontons in cold water; cover with iced water to keep them from sticking together.

Remove bones and skin from chicken; cut chicken into thin slices. Toss chicken, ½ teaspoon cornstarch, ½ teaspoon salt and dash of white pepper in glass or plastic bowl. Cover and refrigerate 20 minutes. Remove strings from pea pods. Place pea pods in boiling water. Cover and cook 1 minute; drain. Immediately rinse under running cold

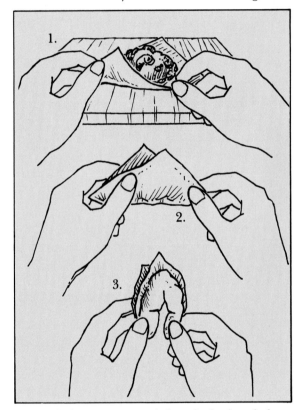

water; drain. Cut pea pods lengthwise into halves. Cut mushrooms into ¼-inch slices.

Heat chicken broth and mushrooms to boiling in 3-quart saucepan. Stir in chicken; heat to boiling. Drain wontons. Stir wontons, bamboo shoots, 1 teaspoon salt and dash of white pepper into chicken broth. Heat to boiling; reduce heat. Simmer uncovered 2 minutes. Stir in pea pods, 2 tablespoons green onions and ¼ teaspoon sesame oil. *8 servings (about 1 cup each).*

Do-ahead Directions: Prepare Wonton Soup; cover and refrigerate no longer than 24 hours. Just before serving, heat soup until hot.

Sam See Soup

Sam See Soup

6   medium dried black mushrooms
1   whole chicken breast (about 1 pound)
½   teaspoon cornstarch
½   teaspoon salt

4   ounces pea pods
2   ounces fully cooked smoked ham
2   whole canned abalone, drained
2   green onions (with tops)

4   cups chicken broth
½   cup shredded canned bamboo shoots
2   teaspoons salt
¼   teaspoon sesame oil
⅛   teaspoon white pepper

Soak mushrooms in warm water until soft, about 30 minutes; drain. Rinse in warm water; drain. Remove and discard stems; cut caps into thin slices. Remove bones and skin from chicken; cut chicken into thin strips. Toss chicken, cornstarch and ½

teaspoon salt in glass or plastic bowl. Cover and refrigerate 20 minutes.

Remove strings from pea pods. Place pea pods in boiling water. Cover and cook 1 minute; drain. Immediately rinse under running cold water; drain. Cut pea pods lengthwise into thin strips. Cut ham and abalone into thin strips. Cut green onions into 2-inch pieces.

Heat chicken broth and mushrooms to boiling in 3-quart saucepan. Stir in chicken and bamboo shoots; heat to boiling. Stir in ham, 2 teaspoons salt, the sesame oil and white pepper. Heat to boiling; reduce heat. Cover and simmer 5 minutes. Add pea pods; cook and stir 30 seconds. Remove from heat; stir in abalone and green onions. *6 servings (about 1 cup each).*

Bok Choy and Fish Ball Soup

1   cup water
3   slices bacon, finely chopped
½   pound fish fillets, finely chopped
4   canned water chestnuts, finely chopped
1   large green onion (with top), finely chopped
1   teaspoon cornstarch
1   teaspoon salt
¼   teaspoon grated gingerroot
¼   teaspoon white pepper
¼   teaspoon sesame oil
3   large stalks bok choy or celery cabbage

4   cups chicken broth
4   thin slices gingerroot
1   teaspoon salt

Heat water to boiling; add bacon. Heat to boiling. Cook uncovered 3 minutes; drain. Mix bacon, fish, water chestnuts, green onion, cornstarch, 1 teaspoon salt, the grated gingerroot, white pepper and sesame oil. Shape mixture into 1-inch balls. Cut bok choy (with leaves) into ½-inch slices.

Heat chicken broth to boiling in 3-quart saucepan. Add fish balls and gingerroot. Heat to boiling; stir in bok choy and 1 teaspoon salt. Heat to boiling; reduce heat. Simmer uncovered 2 minutes. Remove gingerroot. *5 servings (about 1 cup each).*

Lettuce and Fish Soup

½ pound walleye fillets
2 teaspoons vegetable oil
1 teaspoon cornstarch
½ teaspoon salt
½ teaspoon soy sauce
¼ teaspoon sesame oil
  Dash of white pepper
½ head iceberg lettuce

4 cups chicken broth
1 teaspoon salt
1 green onion (with top), chopped

Cut fish crosswise into ½-inch slices. Toss fish, vegetable oil, cornstarch, ½ teaspoon salt, the soy sauce, sesame oil and white pepper in glass or plastic quart bowl. Cover and refrigerate 30 minutes. Remove core from lettuce; cut lettuce into 8 pieces.

Heat chicken broth to boiling in 3-quart saucepan. Add lettuce and 1 teaspoon salt; heat to boiling. Stir in fish. Heat to boiling; remove from heat. Stir in green onion. *5 servings (about 1 cup each).*

Hot and Sour Soup

6 medium dried black mushrooms
¼ pound pork boneless loin
½ teaspoon cornstarch
½ teaspoon salt
½ teaspoon soy sauce (light or dark)
4 to 6 ounces bean curd

4 cups chicken broth
3 tablespoons white vinegar
1 tablespoon soy sauce (light or dark)
1 teaspoon salt
½ cup shredded canned bamboo shoots

2 tablespoons cornstarch
2 tablespoons cold water
¼ teaspoon white pepper
2 eggs, slightly beaten
2 tablespoons chopped green onions (with tops)
2 teaspoons red pepper sauce
½ teaspoon sesame oil

Soak mushrooms in warm water until soft, about 30 minutes; drain. Rinse in warm water; drain.

Remove and discard stems; cut caps into thin slices. Trim fat from pork; shred pork (see page 33). Toss pork, ½ teaspoon cornstarch, ½ teaspoon salt and ½ teaspoon soy sauce in glass or plastic bowl. Cover and refrigerate 15 minutes. Cut bean curd into pieces, 1½ × ¼ inch.

Heat chicken broth, vinegar, 1 tablespoon soy sauce and 1 teaspoon salt to boiling in 3-quart saucepan. Stir in bamboo shoots, mushrooms, pork and bean curd. Heat to boiling; reduce heat. Cover and simmer 5 minutes.

Mix 2 tablespoons cornstarch, the water and white pepper; stir into soup. Heat to boiling, stirring constantly. Pour egg slowly into soup, stirring constantly with fork until egg forms shreds. Stir in green onions, pepper sauce and sesame oil. *5 servings (about 1 cup each).*

Fun See Soup

6 medium dried black mushrooms
2 ounces cellophane noodles (bean threads)
½ pound pork boneless loin

4 cups chicken broth
½ teaspoon cornstarch
½ teaspoon salt
¼ cup shredded canned bamboo shoots
½ cup shredded fully cooked smoked ham
1 teaspoon salt
¼ teaspoon sesame oil
  Dash of white pepper

Soak mushrooms in warm water until soft, about 30 minutes; drain. Rinse in warm water; drain. Remove and discard stems; shred caps finely. Soak noodles in warm water 15 minutes; drain. Cut noodles into 3- to 4-inch pieces. Trim fat from pork; shred pork (see page 33).

Heat chicken broth to boiling in 3-quart saucepan. Toss pork, cornstarch and ½ teaspoon salt; stir into broth. Add mushrooms and bamboo shoots; heat to boiling. Stir in noodles, ham, 1 teaspoon salt, the sesame oil and white pepper. Heat to boiling; reduce heat. Simmer uncovered 5 minutes. *5 servings (about 1 cup each).*

Beef

Stir-fried Beef with Asparagus

10	medium dried black mushrooms*
1	pound beef flank or boneless sirloin steak
1	tablespoon vegetable oil
1	teaspoon cornstarch
1	teaspoon salt
1	teaspoon sugar
1	teaspoon soy sauce (light or dark)
	Dash of white pepper
1	pound asparagus
4	ounces pea pods
2	green onions (with tops)
1/4	cup chicken broth or cold water
2	tablespoons cornstarch
2	tablespoons oyster sauce
1	teaspoon sugar
3	tablespoons vegetable oil
1	teaspoon finely chopped gingerroot
1	teaspoon finely chopped garlic
2	tablespoons vegetable oil
1	teaspoon salt
2	tablespoons dry white wine
1/2	cup chicken broth

*1 cup sliced fresh mushrooms can be substituted for the cut-up rehydrated black mushrooms.

Soak mushrooms in warm water until soft, about 30 minutes; drain. Rinse in warm water; drain. Remove and discard stems; cut caps into 1/2-inch pieces. Trim fat from beef; cut beef with grain into 2-inch strips. Cut strips across grain into 1/8-inch slices. Toss beef, 1 tablespoon vegetable oil, 1 teaspoon cornstarch, 1 teaspoon salt, 1 teaspoon sugar, the soy sauce and white pepper in glass or plastic bowl. Cover and refrigerate 20 minutes.

Break off tough ends of asparagus as far down as stalks snap easily. Cut asparagus into 2-inch pieces. Remove strings from pea pods. Place pea pods in boiling water. Cover and cook 1 minute; drain. Immediately rinse under running cold water; drain. Cut green onions into 2-inch pieces; cut pieces lengthwise into thin strips. Mix 1/4 cup chicken broth, 2 tablespoons cornstarch, the oyster sauce and 1 teaspoon sugar.

Heat wok until 1 or 2 drops of water bubble and skitter when sprinkled in wok. Add 3 tablespoons vegetable oil; rotate wok to coat side. Add beef, gingerroot and garlic; stir-fry until beef is brown, about 3 minutes. Remove beef from wok.

Add 2 tablespoons vegetable oil to wok; rotate to coat side. Add mushrooms, asparagus and 1 teaspoon salt; stir-fry 1 minute. Add wine; cook and stir 30 seconds. Stir in 1/2 cup chicken broth; heat to boiling. Stir in beef; heat to boiling. Stir in cornstarch mixture; cook and stir until thickened, about 20 seconds. Add pea pods; cook and stir 30 seconds. Garnish with green onions. *5 servings.*

Microwave Reheat Directions: Prepare Beef with Asparagus as directed except — omit green onions; cover and refrigerate no longer than 48 hours. Just before serving, prepare green onions. Cover beef mixture tightly and microwave on microwaveproof platter or bowl on high (100%) power 4 minutes; stir. Cover and microwave until hot, about 4 minutes longer. Garnish with green onions.

Stir-fried Beef with Asparagus

Stir-fried Beef with Bok Choy

1   pound beef flank or boneless sirloin steak
1   tablespoon vegetable oil
1   teaspoon cornstarch
1   teaspoon salt
1   teaspoon sugar
1   teaspoon soy sauce (light or dark)
⅛   teaspoon white pepper

1   pound bok choy (about 7 large stalks)
2   green onions (with tops)
2   tablespoons cornstarch
2   tablespoons cold water

3   tablespoons vegetable oil
1   teaspoon finely chopped gingerroot
1   teaspoon finely chopped garlic

3   tablespoons vegetable oil
½   teaspoon salt
½   cup chicken broth
2   tablespoons oyster sauce or 1 tablespoon dark
        soy sauce

Trim fat from beef; cut beef with grain into 2-inch strips. Cut strips across grain into ⅛-inch slices. Toss beef, 1 tablespoon vegetable oil, 1 teaspoon cornstarch, 1 teaspoon salt, the sugar, soy sauce and white pepper in glass or plastic bowl. Cover and refrigerate 30 minutes.

Separate bok choy leaves from stems. Cut leaves into 2-inch pieces; cut stems diagonally into ¼-inch slices (do not combine leaves and stems). Cut green onions into 2-inch pieces. Mix 2 tablespoons cornstarch and the water.

Heat wok until 1 or 2 drops of water bubble and skitter when sprinkled in wok. Add 3 tablespoons vegetable oil; rotate wok to coat side. Add beef, gingerroot and garlic; stir-fry until beef is brown, about 3 minutes. Remove beef from wok.

Add 3 tablespoons vegetable oil to wok; rotate to coat side. Add bok choy stems; stir-fry 1 minute. Stir in bok choy leaves and ½ teaspoon salt. Stir in chicken broth; heat to boiling. Stir in cornstarch mixture; cook and stir until thickened, about 15 seconds. Stir in beef and oyster sauce; heat to boiling. Garnish with green onions. *5 servings.*

Stir-fried Beef with Zucchini

1   pound beef flank or boneless sirloin steak
1   tablespoon vegetable oil
1   teaspoon cornstarch
1   teaspoon salt
1   teaspoon soy sauce (light or dark)
    Dash of white pepper

1   pound zucchini
1   medium onion
1   tablespoon cornstarch
1   tablespoon cold water

3   tablespoons vegetable oil
1   teaspoon finely chopped garlic

3   tablespoons vegetable oil
1   tablespoon soy sauce (light or dark)
1   teaspoon salt
½   cup chicken broth or water

Trim fat from beef; cut beef with grain into 2-inch strips. Cut strips across grain into ⅛-inch slices. Toss beef, 1 tablespoon vegetable oil, 1 teaspoon cornstarch, 1 teaspoon salt, 1 teaspoon soy sauce and the white pepper in glass or plastic bowl. Cover and refrigerate 20 minutes.

Cut zucchini lengthwise into halves; cut each half diagonally into ¼-inch slices. Cut onion into halves. Place each half cut side down; cut into thin slices. Mix 1 tablespoon cornstarch and the water.

Heat wok until 1 or 2 drops of water bubble and skitter when sprinkled in wok. Add 3 tablespoons vegetable oil; rotate wok to coat side. Add beef and garlic; stir-fry until beef is brown, about 3 minutes. Remove beef from wok.

Add 3 tablespoons vegetable oil to wok; rotate to coat side. Add onion; stir-fry until tender, about 2 minutes. Add zucchini; stir-fry 1 minute. Stir in 1 tablespoon soy sauce and 1 teaspoon salt. Stir in chicken broth; heat to boiling. Stir in beef; heat to boiling. Stir in cornstarch mixture; cook and stir until thickened, about 20 seconds. *5 servings.*

Stir-fried Beef with Pea Pods

1   *pound beef flank or boneless sirloin steak*
1   *tablespoon vegetable oil*
1   *teaspoon cornstarch*
1   *teaspoon salt*
1   *teaspoon sugar*
1   *teaspoon soy sauce (light or dark)*
1/8   *teaspoon white pepper*

8   *medium dried black mushrooms**
8   *ounces pea pods*
2   *green onions (with tops)*
1/4   *cup cold water*
2   *tablespoons oyster sauce or 1 tablespoon soy sauce*
      (light or dark)
1   *tablespoon cornstarch*

3   *tablespoons vegetable oil*
1   *teaspoon finely chopped gingerroot*
1   *teaspoon finely chopped garlic*

2   *tablespoons vegetable oil*
1   *can (8½ ounces) sliced bamboo shoots, drained*
1/2   *cup chicken broth*

*1 jar (4½ ounces) sliced mushrooms, drained, can be substituted for the black mushrooms.

Trim fat from beef; cut beef with grain into 2-inch strips. Cut strips across grain into ⅛-inch slices. Toss beef, 1 tablespoon vegetable oil, 1 teaspoon cornstarch, the salt, sugar, soy sauce and white pepper in glass or plastic bowl. Cover and refrigerate 30 minutes.

Soak mushrooms in warm water until soft, about 30 minutes; drain. Rinse in warm water; drain. Remove and discard stems; cut caps into ½-inch pieces. Remove strings from pea pods. Place pea pods in boiling water. Cover and cook 1 minute; drain. Immediately rinse under running cold water; drain. Cut green onions into 2-inch pieces; cut pieces lengthwise into thin strips. Mix water, oyster sauce and 1 tablespoon cornstarch.

Heat wok until 1 or 2 drops of water bubble and skitter when sprinkled in wok. Add 3 tablespoons vegetable oil; rotate wok to coat side. Add beef, gingerroot and garlic; stir-fry until beef is brown, about 3 minutes. Remove beef from wok.

Add 2 tablespoons vegetable oil to wok; rotate to coat side. Add mushrooms and bamboo shoots; stir-fry 1 minute. Stir in chicken broth; heat to boiling. Stir in beef; heat to boiling. Stir in cornstarch mixture; cook and stir until thickened, about 30 seconds. Add pea pods; cook and stir 30 seconds. Garnish with green onions. *5 servings.*

Microwave Reheat Directions: Prepare Beef and Pea Pods as directed except — omit green onions; cover and refrigerate no longer than 48 hours. Just before serving, prepare green onions. Cover beef mixture tightly and microwave on microwaveproof platter or bowl on high (100%) power 4 minutes; stir. Cover and microwave until hot, about 4 minutes longer. Garnish with green onions.

Slicing and Shredding Meat

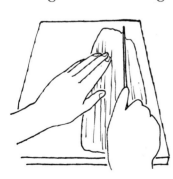

1. Cut meat with the grain into long strips about 2 inches wide.

2. Cut each strip across grain into ⅛-inch slices.

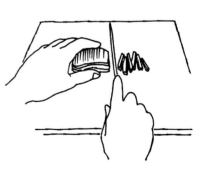

3. To shred meat, stack slices and cut into thin strips.

Stir-fried Beef with Celery

1   pound beef flank or boneless sirloin steak
1   tablespoon vegetable oil
1   teaspoon cornstarch
1   teaspoon salt
1   teaspoon sugar
1   teaspoon soy sauce (light or dark)
1/8 teaspoon white pepper

1/2 bunch celery (about 6 large stalks)
2   green onions (with tops)
1   tablespoon cornstarch
1   tablespoon cold water

3   tablespoons vegetable oil
1   teaspoon finely chopped gingerroot
1   teaspoon finely chopped garlic

3   tablespoons vegetable oil
1/2 cup chicken broth
1/2 teaspoon salt
2   tablespoons dark soy sauce

Trim fat from beef; cut beef with grain into 2-inch strips. Cut strips across grain into 1/8-inch slices. Toss beef, 1 tablespoon vegetable oil, 1 teaspoon cornstarch, 1 teaspoon salt, the sugar, 1 teaspoon soy sauce and the white pepper in glass or plastic bowl. Cover and refrigerate 30 minutes.

Cut celery diagonally into 1/4-inch slices. Cut green onions into 2-inch pieces. Mix 1 tablespoon cornstarch and the water.

Heat wok until 1 or 2 drops of water bubble and skitter when sprinkled in wok. Add 3 tablespoons vegetable oil; rotate wok to coat side. Add beef, gingerroot and garlic; stir-fry until beef is brown, about 3 minutes. Remove beef from wok.

Add 3 tablespoons vegetable oil to wok; rotate. Add celery; stir-fry 1 minute. Stir in chicken broth and 1/2 teaspoon salt; heat to boiling. Cover and cook 2 minutes. Stir in cornstarch mixture; cook and stir until thickened, about 10 seconds. Stir in beef and 2 tablespoons soy sauce; heat to boiling. Garnish with green onions. *4 servings.*

Stir-fried Beef with Green Beans

3/4 pound beef flank or boneless sirloin steak
1   tablespoon vegetable oil
1   teaspoon cornstarch
1   teaspoon soy sauce (light or dark)
1/2 teaspoon salt
    Dash of white pepper

1   pound green beans
2   green onions (with tops)
2   tablespoons cornstarch
2   tablespoons cold water

3   tablespoons vegetable oil
1   medium onion, thinly sliced
1   clove garlic, finely chopped

3   tablespoons vegetable oil
1   teaspoon salt
1/2 cup chicken broth
1   tablespoon dark soy sauce

Trim fat from beef; cut beef with grain into 2-inch strips. Cut strips across grain into 1/8-inch slices. Toss beef, 1 tablespoon vegetable oil, 1 teaspoon cornstarch, 1 teaspoon soy sauce, 1/2 teaspoon salt and the white pepper in glass or plastic bowl. Cover and refrigerate 20 minutes.

Remove ends from beans. Cut beans into 2-inch pieces. Cut green onions into 2-inch pieces. Mix 2 tablespoons cornstarch and the water.

Heat wok until 1 or 2 drops of water bubble and skitter when sprinkled in wok. Add 3 tablespoons vegetable oil; rotate wok to coat side. Add beef; onion slices and garlic; stir-fry until beef is brown, about 3 minutes. Remove beef mixture from wok.

Add 3 tablespoons vegetable oil to wok; rotate to coat side. Add beans and 1 teaspoon salt; stir-fry 2 minutes. Stir in chicken broth; heat to boiling. Cover and cook 2 minutes. Stir in beef; heat to boiling. Stir in cornstarch mixture; cook and stir until thickened, about 15 seconds. Stir in green onions and 1 tablespoon soy sauce; heat to boiling. *5 servings.*

Stir-fried Beef with Broccoli

8   medium dried black mushrooms
1   pound beef flank or tenderloin steak
1   tablespoon vegetable oil
1   teaspoon cornstarch
1   teaspoon salt
1   teaspoon sugar
1   teaspoon soy sauce (light or dark)
1/8   teaspoon white pepper

1 1/2   pounds broccoli
2   green onions (with tops)
1/4   cup chicken broth or cold water
1/4   cup oyster sauce
2   tablespoons cornstarch

3   tablespoons vegetable oil
1   teaspoon finely chopped gingerroot
1   teaspoon finely chopped garlic

2   tablespoons vegetable oil
1/2   teaspoon salt
1/2   cup chicken broth

Soak mushrooms in warm water until soft, about 30 minutes; drain. Rinse in warm water; drain. Remove and discard stems; cut caps into 1/2-inch pieces. Trim fat from beef; cut beef with grain into 2-inch strips. Cut strips across grain into 1/8-inch slices. Toss beef, 1 tablespoon vegetable oil, 1 teaspoon cornstarch, 1 teaspoon salt, sugar, soy sauce and white pepper in glass or plastic bowl. Cover and refrigerate 20 minutes.

Cut broccoli into 1-inch pieces. Cut lengthwise gashes in stems thicker than 1 inch. Place broccoli in boiling water. Cover and cook 1 minute; drain. Immediately rinse under running cold water;

drain. Cut green onions into 2-inch pieces. Mix 1/4 cup chicken broth, the oyster sauce and 2 tablespoons cornstarch.

Heat wok until 1 or 2 drops of water bubble and skitter when sprinkled in wok. Add 3 tablespoons vegetable oil; rotate wok to coat side. Add beef, gingerroot and garlic; stir-fry until beef is brown, about 3 minutes. Remove beef from wok.

Add 2 tablespoons vegetable oil to wok; rotate to coat side. Add mushrooms, broccoli and 1/2 teaspoon salt; stir-fry 1 minute. Stir in 1/2 cup chicken broth; heat to boiling. Stir in beef; heat to boiling. Stir in cornstarch mixture; cook and stir until thickened, about 15 seconds. Garnish with green onions. *7 servings.*

Microwave Reheat Directions: **Prepare Beef with Broccoli as directed except — omit green onions; cover and refrigerate no longer than 48 hours. Just before serving, prepare green onions. Cover beef mixture tightly and microwave on microwaveproof platter or bowl on high (100%) power 4 minutes; stir. Cover and microwave until hot, about 6 minutes longer. Garnish with green onions.**

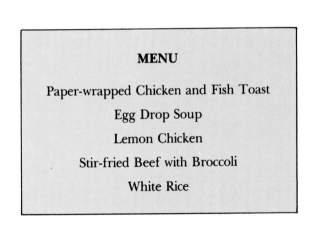

MENU

Paper-wrapped Chicken and Fish Toast

Egg Drop Soup

Lemon Chicken

Stir-fried Beef with Broccoli

White Rice

Pepper Steak

1   pound beef flank or boneless sirloin steak
1   tablespoon vegetable oil
1   teaspoon cornstarch
1   teaspoon salt
1   teaspoon soy sauce (light or dark)
    Dash of white pepper

3   small tomatoes
2   medium green peppers
1   medium onion
¼   cup chicken broth
2   tablespoons cornstarch
2   tablespoons dark soy sauce
1   teaspoon sugar

3   tablespoons vegetable oil
1   teaspoon finely chopped gingerroot
1   teaspoon finely chopped garlic

2   tablespoons vegetable oil
½   cup chicken broth

Trim fat from beef; cut beef with grain into 2-inch strips. Cut strips across grain into ⅛-inch slices. Toss beef, 1 tablespoon vegetable oil, 1 teaspoon cornstarch, the salt, 1 teaspoon soy sauce and white pepper in glass bowl. Refrigerate 30 minutes.

Cut each tomato into 8 wedges. Cut green peppers into 1-inch pieces. Cut onion into ¾-inch pieces. Mix ¼ cup chicken broth, 2 tablespoons cornstarch, 2 tablespoons soy sauce and the sugar.

Heat wok until 2 drops of water bubble and skitter. Add 3 tablespoons vegetable oil; rotate to coat. Add onion, gingerroot and garlic; stir-fry until garlic is light brown. Add beef; stir-fry until beef is brown, about 3 minutes. Remove beef from wok.

Add 2 tablespoons vegetable oil; rotate to coat side. Add tomatoes; stir-fry 30 seconds. Stir in ½ cup chicken broth; heat to boiling. Stir in cornstarch mixture; cook and stir until thickened. Add green peppers and beef; stir-fry 30 seconds. *6 servings.*

Microwave Reheat Directions: Prepare Pepper Steak as directed except — omit tomatoes and green peppers; cover and refrigerate no longer than 48 hours. To serve, prepare tomatoes and green peppers. Cover beef mixture tightly and microwave on microwaveproof platter on high (100%) power 5 minutes; stir in tomatoes and green peppers. Cover and microwave until hot, about 4 minutes.

Pepper Steak

Sweet and Sour Beef

¾ pound beef flank steak
1 egg, slightly beaten
1 tablespoon cornstarch
1 tablespoon vegetable oil
1 teaspoon salt
1 teaspoon soy sauce (light or dark)
¼ teaspoon white pepper
1 medium carrot
1 small green pepper

   Vegetable oil
¼ cup all-purpose flour
¼ cup water
1 tablespoon cornstarch
2 teaspoons vegetable oil
¼ teaspoon baking soda

1 cup sugar
¾ cup chicken broth
¾ cup white vinegar
1 tablespoon vegetable oil
2 teaspoons dark soy sauce
1 teaspoon salt
1 clove garlic, finely chopped
¼ cup cold water
3 tablespoons cornstarch
1 can (8¼ ounces) pineapple chunks, drained

Trim fat from beef; cut beef with grain into 2-inch strips. Cut strips across grain into ⅛-inch slices. Mix egg, 1 tablespoon cornstarch, 1 tablespoon vegetable oil, 1 teaspoon salt, 1 teaspoon soy sauce and the white pepper in glass or plastic bowl; stir in beef. Cover and refrigerate 20 minutes. Cut carrot diagonally into thin slices. Place carrot slices in boiling water. Cover and cook 1 minute; drain. Immediately rinse under cold water; drain. Cut green pepper into 1-inch pieces.

Heat vegetable oil (1½ inches) in wok to 350°. Mix flour, ¼ cup water, 1 tablespoon cornstarch, 2 teaspoons vegetable oil and the baking soda. Stir beef slices into batter until well coated. Fry ¼ of the slices at a time until light brown, turning 2 or 3 times, about 2 minutes. Drain on paper towel. Increase oil temperature to 375°. Fry beef all at one time until golden brown, about 1 minute. Drain on paper towel. Place beef on heated platter.

Heat sugar, chicken broth, vinegar, 1 tablespoon vegetable oil, 2 teaspoons soy sauce, 1 teaspoon salt and the garlic to boiling in 3-quart saucepan. Mix ¼ cup water and 3 tablespoons cornstarch; stir into

Sweet and Sour Beef

sauce. Cook and stir until thickened, about 15 seconds. Stir in carrot, green pepper and pineapple. Heat to boiling; pour over beef. *6 servings.*

Do-ahead Directions: After frying beef 2 minutes, wrap, label and freeze no longer than 1 week. Prepare sauce as directed except — omit green pepper; freeze no longer than 1 week. Just before serving, prepare green pepper. Dip container of sauce into very hot water just to loosen. Place frozen block in 3-quart saucepan. Cover tightly; heat, stirring occasionally, until thawed. Heat frozen beef uncovered in 400° oven until hot, 10 to 12 minutes. Drain on paper towel. Stir green pepper into sauce. Heat to boiling; pour over beef.

Mandarin Beef

Mandarin Beef

1 pound beef boneless round or sirloin steak
1 tablespoon vegetable oil
2 teaspoons cornstarch
1 teaspoon salt
1 teaspoon soy sauce (light or dark)
½ teaspoon sugar
¼ teaspoon white pepper
2 green onions (with tops)
1 large green pepper

¼ cup vegetable oil
1 teaspoon finely chopped gingerroot
1 teaspoon finely chopped garlic
¾ cup shredded carrot
1 to 2 teaspoons chili paste*
1 tablespoon dark soy sauce

*1 teaspoon finely chopped dried chili pepper and 1 tablespoon soy sauce can be substituted for the chili paste.

Trim fat from beef; shred beef (see page 33). Toss beef, 1 tablespoon vegetable oil, the cornstarch, salt, 1 teaspoon soy sauce, the sugar and white pepper in glass or plastic bowl. Cover and refrigerate 30 minutes. Cut green onions into 2-inch pieces. Cut green pepper into ⅛-inch strips.

Heat wok until 1 or 2 drops of water bubble and skitter when sprinkled in wok. Add ¼ cup vegetable oil; rotate wok to coat side. Add beef, gingerroot and garlic; stir-fry until beef is brown, about 3 minutes. Add green pepper, carrot and chili paste; stir-fry 1 minute. Stir in green onions and 1 tablespoon soy sauce; cook and stir 30 seconds. *2 to 3 servings.*

Microwave Reheat Directions: Prepare Mandarin Beef, cover and refrigerate no longer than 24 hours. Cover tightly and microwave on microwaveproof platter or bowl on high (100%) power 4 minutes; stir. Cover and microwave until hot, about 2 minutes longer.

Steamed Beef with Mushrooms

1   pound beef flank or boneless sirloin steak
2   tablespoons vegetable oil
2   teaspoons cornstarch
1   teaspoon salt
1   teaspoon sugar
1   teaspoon finely chopped gingerroot
1   teaspoon light soy sauce
2   green onions (with tops)

1   jar (4½ ounces) sliced mushrooms, drained

Trim fat from beef; cut beef with grain into 2-inch strips. Cut strips across grain into ⅛-inch slices. Toss beef, vegetable oil, cornstarch, salt, sugar, gingerroot and soy sauce in glass or plastic bowl. Cover and refrigerate 30 minutes. Cut green onions into 2-inch pieces; cut pieces lengthwise into thin strips.

Mix beef and mushrooms; place in ungreased 9-inch pie plate or other heatproof plate. Place plate on rack in steamer; cover and steam over boiling water 20 minutes. (Add boiling water if necessary.) Garnish with onions. *2 or 3 servings.*

To Microwave: Cover marinated beef and mushrooms tightly in ungreased microwaveproof round baking dish, 9 × 1½ inches, and microwave on high (100%) power 4 minutes; stir. Cover and microwave until meat is tender, about 3 minutes. Let stand covered 3 minutes. Garnish with onions.

Mongolian Beef

1   pound beef boneless sirloin steak
1   tablespoon cornstarch
1   tablespoon vegetable oil
1   teaspoon salt
1   teaspoon sugar
1   teaspoon soy sauce (light or dark)
    Dash of white pepper
1   green onion (with top)

3   tablespoons vegetable oil
1   teaspoon finely chopped gingerroot
1   teaspoon finely chopped garlic
1   tablespoon dark soy sauce

Trim fat from beef; cut beef with grain into 2-inch strips. Cut strips across grain into ⅛-inch slices. Toss beef, cornstarch, 1 tablespoon vegetable oil, the salt, sugar, 1 teaspoon soy sauce and the white pepper in glass or plastic bowl. Cover and refrigerate 1 hour. Cut green onion into 2-inch pieces.

Heat wok until 1 or 2 drops of water bubble and skitter when sprinkled in wok. Add 3 tablespoons vegetable oil; rotate wok to coat side. Add gingerroot and garlic; stir-fry until brown. Add beef; stir-fry until beef is brown, about 3 minutes. Add 1 tablespoon soy sauce; stir to coat beef. Add green onion; stir-fry 30 seconds. *2 or 3 servings.*

Pork

Stir-fried Spareribs with Green Peppers

2   to 3-pound rack pork ribs, cut lengthwise
      across bones into halves
2   teaspoons cornstarch
2   teaspoons soy sauce (light or dark)
1   teaspoon salt
1   teaspoon sugar
2   green peppers
2   green onions (with tops)

2   tablespoons vegetable oil
2   cloves garlic, finely chopped
1   teaspoon finely chopped gingerroot
2   tablespoons brown bean sauce
1   cup chicken broth

1/4   cup cold water
2   tablespoons cornstarch
1   teaspoon sugar

Trim fat and remove membranes from ribs; cut between each rib to separate. Toss ribs, 2 teaspoons cornstarch, the soy sauce, salt and 1 teaspoon sugar in glass or plastic bowl. Cover and refrigerate 30 minutes. Cut green peppers into 1-inch pieces. Cut green onions into 2-inch pieces.

Heat wok until 1 or 2 drops of water bubble and skitter when sprinkled in wok. Add vegetable oil; rotate wok to coat side. Add ribs, garlic and gingerroot; stir-fry 2 minutes. Add bean sauce; stir-fry 1 minute. Stir in chicken broth. Heat to boiling; reduce heat. Cover and simmer 20 minutes.

Mix water, 2 tablespoons cornstarch and 1 teaspoon sugar; stir into ribs. Cook and stir until thickened. Add green peppers; cook and stir 1 minute. Garnish with green onions. *3 or 4 servings.*

Do-ahead Directions: After simmering ribs 20 minutes, cover and refrigerate no longer than 24 hours. Just before serving, heat ribs to boiling; cover and cook 2 minutes. Continue as directed.

Stir-fried Pork with Cauliflower

1   pound pork boneless loin or leg
1   teaspoon cornstarch
1   teaspoon salt
1   teaspoon light soy sauce
1/2 teaspoon sugar
      Dash of white pepper

1   small cauliflower (about 1 pound)
3   green onions (with tops)
2   tablespoons cornstarch
2   tablespoons cold water

3   tablespoons vegetable oil
1   small onion, thinly sliced
1   teaspoon finely chopped garlic
1   tablespoon dark soy sauce
1/2 cup chicken broth
2   tablespoons oyster sauce

Trim fat from pork; cut into slices, $2 \times 1 \times 1/8$ inch. Toss pork, 1 teaspoon cornstarch, the salt, 1 teaspoon soy sauce, the sugar and pepper in glass or plastic bowl. Cover and refrigerate 20 minutes.

Remove outer leaves and stalk from cauliflower. Separate cauliflower into bite-size flowerets. Place cauliflowerets in boiling water. Cover and cook 2 minutes; drain. Immediately rinse under running cold water; drain. Cut green onions into 2-inch pieces. Mix 2 tablespoons cornstarch and the water.

Heat wok until 1 or 2 drops of water bubble and skitter when sprinkled in wok. Add vegetable oil; rotate wok to coat side. Add onion slices; stir-fry until light brown. Add pork and garlic; stir-fry until pork is no longer pink. Stir in cauliflowerets and 1 tablespoon soy sauce. Stir in chicken broth; heat to boiling. Cover and cook 1 minute. Stir in cornstarch mixture; cook and stir until thickened, about 10 seconds. Stir in green onions and oyster sauce. *4 servings.*

Stir-fried Spareribs with Green Peppers

Stir-fried Pork with Cabbage (Szechwan Style)

1   pound pork boneless loin or leg
1   teaspoon cornstarch
1   teaspoon soy sauce
½   teaspoon salt
⅛   teaspoon white pepper

8   ounces cabbage (about ¼ head)
2   green onions (with tops)
1   small green pepper
2   teaspoons cornstarch
2   teaspoons cold water
¼   cup vegetable oil
1   clove garlic, finely chopped
2   teaspoons chili paste*
¼   cup chicken broth

*1 teaspoon finely chopped dried chili pepper and 1 tablespoon soy sauce can be substituted for the chili paste.

Trim fat from pork; cut into slices, 2 × 1 × ⅛ inch. Toss pork, 1 teaspoon cornstarch, the soy sauce, salt and white pepper in glass or plastic bowl. Cover and refrigerate 20 minutes.

Cut cabbage into 1-inch pieces. Cut green onions into 2-inch pieces. Cut green pepper into 1-inch pieces. Mix 2 teaspoons cornstarch and the water.

Heat wok until 1 or 2 drops of water bubble and skitter when sprinkled in wok. Add vegetable oil; rotate wok to coat side. Add pork and garlic; stir-fry until pork is no longer pink. Add cabbage and green pepper; stir-fry 2 minutes. Stir in chili paste. Stir in chicken broth; heat to boiling. Stir in cornstarch mixture; cook and stir until thickened, about 10 seconds. Stir in green onions. *4 servings.*

Microwave Reheat Directions: Prepare Stir-fried Pork with Cabbage; cover and refrigerate no longer than 24 hours. Cover tightly and microwave on microwaveproof platter or bowl on high (100%) power 4 minutes; stir. Cover and microwave until hot, about 3 minutes longer.

Stir-fried Pork with Cabbage (Szechwan Style)

Stir-fried Pork with Mixed Vegetables

1¼   pound pork boneless loin or leg
1   teaspoon cornstarch
1   teaspoon salt
1   teaspoon soy sauce (light or dark)
½   teaspoon sugar
    Dash of white pepper

8   ounces bok choy (about 4 large stalks)
4   ounces pea pods
4   ounces mushrooms
2   green onions (with tops)
¼   cup cold water
2   tablespoons cornstarch

¼   cup vegetable oil
1   teaspoon finely chopped gingerroot
1   teaspoon finely chopped garlic
2   tablespoons dry white wine
2   tablespoons oyster sauce
1   teaspoon salt
½   cup chicken broth

Trim fat from pork; cut pork into slices, 2 × 1 × ⅛ inch. Toss pork, 1 teaspoon cornstarch, 1 teaspoon salt, the soy sauce, sugar and white pepper in glass or plastic bowl. Cover and refrigerate 20 minutes.

Separate bok choy leaves from stems. Cut leaves into 2-inch pieces; cut stems diagonally into ¼-inch slices (do not combine leaves and stems). Remove strings from pea pods. Place pea pods in boiling water. Cover and cook 1 minute; drain. Immediately rinse under running cold water; drain. Cut mushrooms into ¼-inch slices. Cut green onions into 2-inch pieces. Mix water and 2 tablespoons cornstarch.

Heat wok until 1 or 2 drops of water bubble and skitter when sprinkled in wok. Add vegetable oil; rotate wok. Add pork, gingerroot and garlic; stir-fry until pork is no longer pink. Add bok choy stems and mushrooms; stir-fry 1 minute. Stir in bok choy leaves, wine, oyster sauce and 1 teaspoon salt. Stir in chicken broth; heat to boiling. Stir in cornstarch mixture; cook and stir until thickened, about 10 seconds. Add pea pods; cook and stir 30 seconds. Garnish with green onions. *5 servings.*

Stir-fried Pork with Straw Mushrooms

1¼   pound pork boneless loin or leg
2   teaspoons cornstarch
1   teaspoon salt
1   teaspoon soy sauce (light or dark)
½   teaspoon sugar
    Dash of white pepper
8   ounces pea pods
3   green onions (with tops)
1   tablespoon cornstarch
1   tablespoon cold water

¼   cup vegetable oil
1   teaspoon finely chopped garlic
2   cans (8 ounces each) straw mushrooms, drained
1   can (8½ ounces) sliced bamboo shoots, drained
1   tablespoon dark soy sauce
¼   cup chicken broth

Trim fat from pork; cut pork into slices, 2 × 1 × ⅛ inch. Toss pork, 2 teaspoons cornstarch, the salt, 1 teaspoon soy sauce, the sugar and white pepper in glass or plastic bowl. Cover and refrigerate 20 minutes. Remove strings from pea pods. Place pea pods in boiling water. Cover and cook 1 minute; drain. Immediately rinse under running cold water; drain. Cut green onions into 2-inch pieces. Mix 1 tablespoon cornstarch and the water.

Heat wok until 1 or 2 drops of water bubble and skitter when sprinkled in wok. Add vegetable oil; rotate wok to coat side. Add pork and garlic; stir-fry until pork is no longer pink. Add mushrooms, bamboo shoots and 1 tablespoon soy sauce; stir-fry 1 minute. Stir in chicken broth; heat to boiling. Stir in cornstarch mixture; cook and stir until thickened, about 10 seconds. Add green onions and pea pods; cook and stir 30 seconds. *6 servings.*

Microwave Reheat Directions: Prepare Stir-fried Pork with Straw Mushrooms; cover and refrigerate no longer than 24 hours. Just before serving, cover tightly and microwave on microwaveproof platter or bowl on high (100%) power 5 minutes; stir. Cover and microwave until hot, about 4 minutes longer. Let stand covered 2 minutes.

Stir-fried Pork with Sweet and Sour Sauce

1¼ pound pork boneless loin or leg
1 teaspoon cornstarch
1 teaspoon salt
1 teaspoon soy sauce (light or dark)
½ teaspoon sugar
    Dash of white pepper
1 medium carrot
1 medium green pepper
2 green onions (with tops)
1 tablespoon cornstarch
1 tablespoon cold water

3 tablespoons vegetable oil
1 clove garlic, finely chopped
⅓ cup chicken broth
1 can (8¼ ounces) pineapple chunks, drained
¼ cup sugar
¼ cup white vinegar
1 tablespoon dark soy sauce

Trim fat from pork; cut pork into slices, $2 \times 1 \times \frac{1}{8}$ inch. Toss pork, 1 teaspoon cornstarch, the salt, 1 teaspoon soy sauce, ½ teaspoon sugar and the white pepper in glass or plastic bowl. Cover and refrigerate 20 minutes. Cut carrot diagonally into thin slices. Cut green pepper into 1-inch pieces. Cut green onions into 2-inch pieces. Mix 1 tablespoon cornstarch and the water.

Heat wok until 1 or 2 drops of water bubble and skitter when sprinkled in wok. Add vegetable oil; rotate wok to coat side. Add garlic; stir-fry until light brown. Add pork; stir-fry until no longer pink. Stir in carrot and chicken broth. Cover and cook over high heat 1 minute. Stir in pineapple. Mix ¼ cup sugar, the vinegar and 1 tablespoon soy sauce; stir into pork mixture. Heat to boiling. Stir in cornstarch mixture; cook and stir until thickened, about 20 seconds. Add green pepper and green onions; cook and stir 30 seconds. *4 servings.*

Microwave Reheat Directions: Prepare Stir-fried Pork with Sweet and Sour Sauce as directed except — omit green pepper and green onions; cover and refrigerate no longer than 24 hours. Just before serving, prepare green pepper and green onions. Cover pork mixture tightly and microwave on microwaveproof platter or bowl on high (100%) power 4 minutes; stir in green pepper and green onions. Cover and microwave until hot, about 4 minutes longer. Let stand covered 2 minutes.

Stir-fried Pork with Fun See

1 pound pork boneless loin or leg
1 teaspoon cornstarch
1 teaspoon salt
1 teaspoon soy sauce (light or dark)
½ teaspoon sugar
⅛ teaspoon white pepper
6 to 8 medium dried black mushrooms
2 green onions (with tops)
2 tablespoons cornstarch
2 tablespoons cold water
3 tablespoons oyster sauce

    Vegetable oil
2 ounces cellophane noodles (bean threads)

3 tablespoons vegetable oil
1 teaspoon finely chopped gingerroot
1 teaspoon finely chopped garlic

2 tablespoons vegetable oil
2 cups thinly sliced celery cabbage
1 cup chicken broth

Trim fat from pork; cut pork into slices, $2 \times 1 \times \frac{1}{8}$ inch. Toss pork, 1 teaspoon cornstarch, the salt, soy sauce, sugar and white pepper in glass or plastic bowl. Cover and refrigerate 30 minutes. Soak mushrooms in warm water until soft, about 30 minutes; drain. Rinse in warm water; drain. Remove and discard stems; shred caps. Cut green onions into 2-inch pieces. Mix 2 tablespoons cornstarch, the water and oyster sauce.

Heat vegetable oil (1 inch) in wok to 425°. Fry ¼ of the noodles at a time until puffed, turning once, about 5 seconds. Drain on paper towel. Wash and dry wok thoroughly.

Heat wok until 2 drops of water bubble and skitter. Add 3 tablespoons vegetable oil; rotate wok. Add pork, gingerroot and garlic; stir-fry until pork is no longer pink. Remove pork from wok.

Add 2 tablespoons oil to wok; rotate. Add mushrooms and celery cabbage; stir-fry 2 minutes. Stir in chicken broth. Cover and cook 2 minutes. Stir in pork; heat to boiling. Stir in cornstarch mixture; cook and stir until thickened. Remove from heat. Stir in onions and half of the noodles. Sprinkle with remaining noodles. *6 servings.*

Do-ahead Tip: Fry cellophane noodles as directed. Store in airtight container at room temperature no longer than 5 days.

Fried Pork with Vegetables

Fried Pork with Vegetables

1   pound pork boneless loin or leg
1   egg, slightly beaten
1   tablespoon cornstarch
1   tablespoon vegetable oil
1/2 teaspoon salt
1/2 teaspoon soy sauce (light or dark)
     Dash of white pepper

1   pound bok choy (about 7 large stalks)
4   ounces pea pods
2   green onions (with tops)
1   tablespoon cornstarch
1   tablespoon cold water

     Vegetable oil
1/3 cup all-purpose flour
1/3 cup water
1 1/2 teaspoons cornstarch
1/2 teaspoon salt
1/2 teaspoon baking soda

3   tablespoons vegetable oil
1   teaspoon finely chopped gingerroot
1   tablespoon dry white wine
1/2 teaspoon salt
1/4 cup chicken broth
1   tablespoon soy sauce (light or dark)

Trim fat from pork; cut pork into ¾-inch pieces. Mix egg, 1 tablespoon cornstarch, 1 tablespoon vegetable oil, ½ teaspoon salt, ½ teaspoon soy sauce and the white pepper in glass or plastic bowl; stir in pork. Cover and refrigerate 30 minutes.

Separate bok choy leaves from stems. Cut leaves into 2-inch pieces; cut stems diagonally into ¼-inch slices (do not combine leaves and stems). Remove strings from pea pods. Place pea pods in boiling water. Cover and cook 1 minute; drain. Immediately rinse under running cold water; drain. Cut green onions into 2-inch pieces. Mix 1 tablespoon cornstarch and 1 tablespoon water.

Heat vegetable oil (1 inch) in wok to 350°. Mix flour, ⅓ cup water, 1½ teaspoons cornstarch, ½ teaspoon salt and the baking soda. Stir pork pieces into batter until well coated. Fry ¼ of the pork pieces at a time until light brown, turning frequently, about 3 minutes. Drain on paper towel. Increase oil temperature to 375°. Fry pork all at one time until golden brown, about 1 minute. Drain on paper towel. Wash and dry wok thoroughly.

Heat wok until 1 or 2 drops of water bubble and skitter when sprinkled in wok. Add 3 tablespoons vegetable oil; rotate wok to coat side. Add bok choy stems and gingerroot; stir-fry 1 minute. Add bok choy leaves, wine and ½ teaspoon salt; stir-fry 1 minute. Stir in chicken broth; heat to boiling. Stir in cornstarch mixture; cook and stir until thickened, about 10 seconds. Stir in pork, pea pods and 1 tablespoon soy sauce. Cook until pork is hot, about 1 minute. Garnish with green onions. *5 servings.*

Mou Shu Pork

Mandarin Pancakes
1¼ pound pork boneless loin or leg
1 teaspoon cornstarch
1 teaspoon salt
1 teaspoon light soy sauce
½ teaspoon sugar
½ teaspoon white pepper
6 large dried black mushrooms
2 green onions (with tops)
2 tablespoons cold water
1 teaspoon cornstarch
1 teaspoon soy sauce (light or dark)

2 tablespoons vegetable oil
1 egg, slightly beaten
¼ teaspoon salt
Dash of white pepper
2 tablespoons vegetable oil
1 teaspoon finely chopped garlic
1 can (8½ ounces) sliced bamboo shoots,
    drained and shredded
¼ cup chicken broth

Prepare Mandarin Pancakes. Trim fat from pork; shred pork (see page 33). Toss pork, 1 teaspoon cornstarch, 1 teaspoon salt, 1 teaspoon soy sauce, the sugar and ½ teaspoon white pepper in glass or plastic bowl. Cover and refrigerate 30 minutes. Soak mushrooms in warm water until soft, about 30 minutes; drain. Rinse in warm water; drain. Remove and discard stems; cut caps into thin slices. Cut green onions into 2-inch pieces. Mix water, 1 teaspoon cornstarch and 1 teaspoon soy sauce.

Heat wok until 1 or 2 drops of water bubble and skitter when sprinkled in wok. Add 2 tablespoons vegetable oil; rotate wok to coat side. Mix egg, ¼ teaspoon salt and dash of white pepper; pour into wok. Rotate wok to coat bottom with egg. Fry egg until firm, turning once, about 10 seconds. Remove egg from wok; cut into thin strips.

Add 2 tablespoons vegetable oil to wok; rotate to coat side. Add garlic; stir-fry until brown. Add pork; stir-fry until no longer pink. Add mushrooms and bamboo shoots; stir-fry 1 minute. Stir in chicken broth; cook and stir 2 minutes. Stir in cornstarch mixture; cook and stir until thickened, about 10 seconds. Add green onions and egg strips; cook and stir 30 seconds.

Each person takes a pancake and spoons about ¼ cup pork mixture onto the center. Fold two oppo-

site sides over filling, overlapping edges about ½ inch in center. Fold one unfolded edge over folded sides to form a pocket. *8 servings.*

Mandarin Pancakes

2¼ cups all-purpose flour
1 cup boiling water
    Sesame oil

Mix flour and water with fork until dough holds together. Turn dough onto lightly floured surface; knead until smooth, about 8 minutes. Shape dough into 8-inch roll; cut roll into eight 1-inch slices. Cut each slice into halves. (Cover pieces of dough with plastic wrap to keep them from drying out.)

Shape each of 2 pieces of dough into a ball; flatten slightly. Roll each ball of dough into a 4-inch circle on lightly floured surface. (1) Brush top of one circle with sesame oil; top with remaining circle. (2) Roll each double circle into a 7-inch circle on lightly floured surface. Repeat with remaining pieces of dough. (Cover circles with plastic wrap to keep them from drying out.)

Heat 8- or 9-inch ungreased skillet over medium heat until warm. (3) Cook one circle at a time, turning frequently, until pancake is blistered with air pockets, turns slightly translucent and feels dry. (Do not overcook or pancake will become brittle.) (4) Carefully separate into 2 pancakes; fold each pancake into fourths. Repeat each step with remaining circles.

Heat pancakes before serving. Place folded pancakes on heatproof plate or rack in steamer; cover and steam over boiling water 10 minutes. (Add boiling water if necessary.) *16 pancakes.*

Do-ahead Directions: After folding each pancake into fourths, cover and refrigerate no longer than 48 hours or wrap, label and freeze no longer than 2 months. Prepare Mou Shu Pork; cover and refrigerate no longer than 24 hours. Just before serving, place refrigerated or frozen pancakes on heatproof plate. Place plate on rack in steamer; cover and steam pancakes over boiling water until hot. Steam refrigerated pancakes 10 minutes, frozen pancakes 12 minutes. Cover pork mixture tightly and microwave on microwaveproof platter or bowl on high (100%) power 2 minutes; stir. Cover and microwave until hot, about 2 minutes longer. Let stand covered 2 minutes.

How to Prepare Mandarin Pancakes

Mou Shu Pork

Steamed Spareribs

2   to 3-pound rack pork ribs, cut lengthwise
        across bones into halves
2   tablespoons salted black beans
2   tablespoons vegetable oil
1   tablespoon cornstarch
1   tablespoon soy sauce (light or dark)
1   teaspoon salt
1   teaspoon finely chopped gingerroot
1   teaspoon finely chopped garlic
1/4 teaspoon white pepper
1/4 teaspoon sesame oil

Trim fat and remove membranes from ribs; cut between each rib to separate. Soak beans in warm water 15 minutes; drain. Rinse beans in cold water to remove skins; drain. Mash beans. Toss ribs, beans and remaining ingredients in glass or plastic bowl. Cover and refrigerate 1 hour.

Place ribs on heatproof plate. Place on rack in steamer; cover and steam over boiling water 30 minutes. (Add boiling water if necessary.) *2 or 3 servings.*

Mandarin Pork

1¼ pound pork boneless loin or leg
1   tablespoon vegetable oil
2   teaspoons cornstarch
1   teaspoon salt
1   teaspoon soy sauce (light or dark)
1/2 teaspoon sugar
1/4 teaspoon white pepper
2   green onions (with tops)
1   large green pepper

1/4 cup vegetable oil
1   teaspoon finely chopped gingerroot
1   teaspoon finely chopped garlic
1   can (8½ ounces) sliced bamboo shoots,
        drained and shredded
3/4 cup shredded carrots
1   tablespoon soy sauce (light or dark)
2   teaspoons chili paste*

*1 teaspoon finely chopped dried chili pepper and 1 tablespoon soy sauce can be substituted for the chili paste.

Trim fat from pork; shred pork (page 33). Toss pork, 1 tablespoon vegetable oil, the cornstarch, salt, 1 teaspoon soy sauce, the sugar and white pepper in glass or plastic bowl. Cover and refrigerate 30 minutes. Cut green onions into 2-inch pieces. Cut green pepper into 1/8-inch strips.

Heat wok until 1 or 2 drops of water bubble and skitter when sprinkled in wok. Add 1/4 cup vegetable oil; rotate wok to coat side. Add pork, gingerroot and garlic; stir-fry until pork is no longer pink. Add green pepper, bamboo shoots and carrots; stir-fry 1 minute. Stir in green onions, 1 tablespoon soy sauce and the chili paste. *5 servings.*

Pork with Bean Curd (Szechwan Style)

3/4 pound ground pork
1   teaspoon cornstarch
1   teaspoon salt
1   teaspoon light soy sauce
1/4 teaspoon sesame oil
1/8 teaspoon white pepper
1   pound bean curd
1   tablespoon cornstarch
1   tablespoon cold water

2   tablespoons vegetable oil
1   teaspoon finely chopped garlic
1   tablespoon dark soy sauce
2   teaspoons chili paste*
1/2 cup chicken broth
2   green onions (with tops)

*1 teaspoon finely chopped dried chili pepper and 1 tablespoon soy sauce can be substituted for the chili paste.

Mix pork, 1 teaspoon cornstarch, the salt, 1 teaspoon soy sauce, the sesame oil and white pepper in glass or plastic bowl. Cover and refrigerate 30 minutes. Cut bean curd into 1/2-inch pieces. Mix 1 tablespoon cornstarch and the water.

Heat wok until 1 or 2 drops of water bubble and skitter when sprinkled in wok; add oil; rotate wok to coat side. Add pork and garlic; stir-fry until pork is no longer pink. Stir in 1 tablespoon soy sauce and the chili paste. Stir in bean curd. Stir in chicken broth; heat to boiling. Stir in cornstarch mixture; cook and stir until thickened, about 20 seconds. Stir in green onions. *4 servings.*

Sweet and Sour Pork

1½ pound pork boneless loin or leg
 1 egg, slightly beaten
 2 tablespoons cornstarch
 2 tablespoons vegetable oil
 1 teaspoon salt
 1 teaspoon light soy sauce
¼ teaspoon white pepper
 2 tomatoes
 1 green pepper

    Vegetable oil
¾ cup all-purpose flour
¾ cup water
 2 tablespoons cornstarch
 1 teaspoon salt
 1 teaspoon baking soda

 1 cup plus 2 tablespoons sugar
 1 cup chicken broth
¾ cup white vinegar
 1 tablespoon vegetable oil
 2 teaspoons dark soy sauce
 1 teaspoon salt
 1 clove garlic, finely chopped
¼ cup cornstarch
¼ cup cold water
 1 can (8¼ ounces) pineapple chunks, drained

Trim fat from pork; cut pork into ¾-inch pieces. Mix egg, 2 tablespoons cornstarch, 2 tablespoons vegetable oil, 1 teaspoon salt, 1 teaspoon soy sauce and the white pepper in glass or plastic bowl; stir in pork. Cover and refrigerate 20 minutes. Cut each tomato into 8 wedges. Cut green pepper into 1-inch pieces.

Heat vegetable oil (1½ inches) in wok to 350°. Mix flour, ¾ cup water, 2 tablespoons cornstarch, 1 teaspoon salt and the baking soda. Stir pork pieces into batter until well coated. Fry about 15 pieces at a time until light brown, turning frequently, 4 minutes. Drain on paper towel. Increase oil temperature to 375°. Fry pork all at one time until golden brown, about 1 minute. Drain on paper towel. Place pork on heated platter.

Heat sugar, chicken broth, vinegar, 1 tablespoon vegetable oil, 2 teaspoons soy sauce, 1 teaspoon salt and the garlic to boiling in 3-quart saucepan. Mix ¼ cup cornstarch and ¼ cup water; stir into sauce. Cook and stir until thickened, about 20 seconds. Stir in tomatoes, green pepper and pineapple. Heat to boiling; pour over pork. *8 servings.*

Do-ahead Directions: After frying pork 4 minutes, wrap, label and freeze no longer than 1 week. Prepare sauce as directed except — omit tomatoes and green pepper; freeze no longer than 1 week. Just before serving, prepare tomatoes and green pepper. Dip container of frozen sauce into very hot water just to loosen. Place frozen block in 3-quart saucepan. Cover tightly; heat, stirring occasionally, until thawed. Heat frozen pork uncovered in 400° oven until hot, about 25 minutes. Drain on paper towel. Stir tomatoes and green pepper into sauce. Heat to boiling; pour over pork.

Chicken & Duck

Lemon Chicken

2   whole chicken breasts (about 2 pounds)
1   tablespoon vegetable oil
1   egg
2   teaspoons cornstarch
1   teaspoon salt
1   teaspoon soy sauce (light or dark)
¼   teaspoon white pepper

    Vegetable oil
¼   cup all-purpose flour
¼   cup water
2   tablespoons cornstarch
2   tablespoons vegetable oil
¼   teaspoon baking soda
¼   teaspoon salt

½   cup chicken broth
¼   cup honey
3   tablespoons lemon juice
2   tablespoons light corn syrup
2   tablespoons vinegar
1   tablespoon vegetable oil
1   tablespoon catsup
1   clove garlic, finely chopped
½   teaspoon salt
    Dash of white pepper
    Peel of ½ lemon
1   tablespoon cornstarch
1   tablespoon cold water
½   lemon, thinly sliced

Remove bones and skin from chicken; cut each breast into fourths. Place chicken in shallow glass or plastic dish. Mix 1 tablespoon vegetable oil, the egg, 2 teaspoons cornstarch, 1 teaspoon salt, the soy sauce and ¼ teaspoon white pepper; pour over chicken. Turn chicken to coat both sides. Cover and refrigerate 30 minutes. Remove chicken from marinade; reserve marinade.

Heat vegetable oil (1½ inches) in wok to 350°. Mix reserved marinade, the flour, ¼ cup water, 2 tablespoons cornstarch, 2 tablespoons vegetable oil, the baking soda and ¼ teaspoon salt. Dip chicken pieces one at a time into batter. Fry 2 pieces at a time until light brown, 3 minutes. Drain on paper towel. Increase oil temperature to 375°. Fry chicken all at one time until golden brown, turning once, about 2 minutes. Drain on paper towel. Cut each piece crosswise into 5 or 6 pieces; place in single layer on heated platter.

Heat chicken broth, honey, lemon juice, corn syrup, vinegar, 1 tablespoon vegetable oil, the catsup, garlic, ½ teaspoon salt, dash of white pepper and the lemon peel to boiling. Mix 1 tablespoon cornstarch and 1 tablespoon water; stir into sauce. Cook and stir until thickened, about 10 seconds. Remove lemon peel. Garnish with lemon slices; pour sauce over chicken. *8 servings.*

Do-ahead Directions: After frying chicken 3 minutes, cover and refrigerate no longer than 24 hours. Prepare sauce (remove lemon peel); cover and refrigerate no longer than 24 hours. Just before serving, prepare lemon slices. Heat vegetable oil (1½ inches) in wok to 375°. Fry chicken all at one time until hot, turning once, 2 minutes. Cut each piece crosswise into 5 or 6 pieces; place in single layer on platter. Heat sauce to boiling, stirring occasionally. Garnish with lemon slices; pour sauce over chicken.

Lemon Chicken

Sweet and Sour Chicken

2½   to 3-pound broiler-fryer chicken, cut up
  1   egg, slightly beaten
  1   tablespoon cornstarch
  2   teaspoons light soy sauce
  1   teaspoon salt
      Dash of white pepper
  2   tomatoes
  1   green pepper

      Vegetable oil
½   cup all-purpose flour
½   cup water
¼   cup cornstarch
  1   tablespoon vegetable oil
½   teaspoon salt
½   teaspoon baking soda

1¼   cups sugar
  1   cup chicken broth
¾   cup white vinegar
  1   tablespoon vegetable oil
  2   teaspoons dark soy sauce
½   teaspoon salt
  1   clove garlic, finely chopped
¼   cup cornstarch
¼   cup cold water
  1   can (8¼ ounces) pineapple chunks, drained

Remove bones and skin from chicken; cut chicken into 1-inch pieces. Mix egg, 1 tablespoon cornstarch, 2 teaspoons soy sauce, 1 teaspoon salt and the white pepper in glass or plastic bowl; stir in chicken. Cover and refrigerate 20 minutes. Cut each tomato into 8 wedges. Cut green pepper into 1-inch pieces.

Heat vegetable oil (1½ inches) in wok to 350°. Mix flour, ½ cup water, ¼ cup cornstarch, 1 tablespoon vegetable oil, ½ teaspoon salt and the baking soda. Stir chicken into batter until well coated. Fry about 15 pieces at a time until light brown, turning frequently, 3 minutes. Drain on paper towel. Increase oil temperature to 375°. Fry chicken all at one time until golden brown, about 1 minute. Drain on paper towel.

Heat sugar, chicken broth, vinegar, 1 tablespoon vegetable oil, 2 teaspoons soy sauce, ½ teaspoon salt and the garlic to boiling in 2-quart saucepan. Mix ¼ cup cornstarch and ¼ cup water; stir into sauce. Cook and stir until thickened, about 10 seconds. Stir in tomatoes, green pepper and pineapple. Heat to boiling; pour over chicken. *6 servings.*

Do-ahead Directions: After frying chicken 3 minutes, wrap, label and freeze no longer than 1 week. Prepare sauce as directed except — omit tomatoes and green pepper; freeze no longer than 1 week. Just before serving, prepare tomatoes and green pepper. Dip container of sauce into hot water to loosen. Place frozen block in saucepan. Cover tightly; heat, stirring occasionally, until thawed. Heat frozen chicken uncovered in 400° oven until hot, about 25 minutes. Stir tomatoes and green pepper into sauce. Heat to boiling; pour over chicken.

Boning and Shredding a Chicken Breast

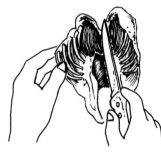

1. Cut only through white gristle at neck end.

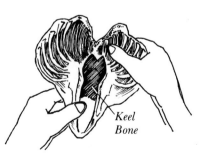

2. Bend back to pop keel bone.

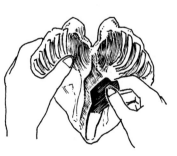

3. Loosen keel; pull from chicken.

Boneless Chicken with Almond Sauce

2 whole chicken breasts (about 2 pounds)
1 egg
1 tablespoon vegetable oil
2 teaspoons cornstarch
1 teaspoon salt
1 teaspoon soy sauce (light or dark)
¼ teaspoon white pepper
2 green onions (with tops)

Vegetable oil
⅓ cup chopped blanched almonds
⅛ teaspoon salt
¼ cup all-purpose flour
¼ cup water
2 tablespoons cornstarch
1½ teaspoons vegetable oil
¼ teaspoon baking soda
¼ teaspoon salt

1½ cups chicken broth
¼ cup shredded canned bamboo shoots
2 teaspoons dark soy sauce
Dash of white pepper
2 tablespoons cornstarch
2 tablespoons cold water

Remove bones and skin from chicken; cut each breast lengthwise into 8 pieces. Mix egg, 1 table-spoon vegetable oil, 2 teaspoons cornstarch, 1 teaspoon salt, 1 teaspoon soy sauce and ¼ teaspoon white pepper in glass or plastic bowl; stir in chicken. Cover and refrigerate 30 minutes. Cut green onions into 2-inch pieces.

Heat vegetable oil (1½ inches) in wok to 350°. Fry almonds until light brown, about 30 seconds. Remove almonds from wok; drain on paper towel. Sprinkle with ⅛ teaspoon salt. Mix flour, ¼ cup water, 2 tablespoons cornstarch, 1½ teaspoons vegetable oil, the baking soda and ¼ teaspoon salt. Dip chicken pieces one at a time into batter. Fry 2 pieces at a time until light brown, about 3 minutes. Drain on paper towel. Increase oil temperature to 375°. Fry chicken all at one time until golden brown, about 4 minutes. Drain on paper towel. Cut each piece crosswise into 5 pieces. Place chicken on heated platter.

Heat chicken broth, bamboo shoots, 2 teaspoons soy sauce and dash of white pepper to boiling. Mix 2 tablespoons cornstarch and 2 tablespoons water; stir into sauce. Cook and stir until thickened, about 1 minute; pour over chicken. Garnish with green onions and almonds. *4 servings.*

Do-ahead Directions: After cutting each piece of fried chicken into 5 pieces, cover and refrigerate no longer than 24 hours. Prepare sauce; cover and refrigerate no longer than 24 hours. Store fried almonds in airtight container at room temperature no longer than 24 hours. Just before serving, prepare green onions. Heat chicken uncovered in 400° oven until hot, 10 to 12 minutes. Heat sauce to boiling; pour over chicken. Garnish with green onions and almonds.

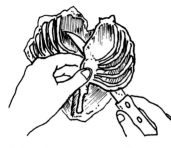

4. Cut rib cages away, cutting through shoulder joint.

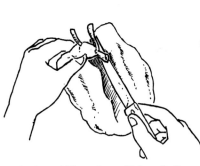

5. Cut wishbone from chicken. Split breast after pulling and cutting the tendons.

6. To shred chicken, cut chicken crosswise into ⅛-inch slices. Stack slices; cut into thin strips.

Steamed Chicken with Black Mushrooms and Tiger Lily Buds

2½ to 3-pound broiler-fryer chicken, cut up
 2 tablespoons vegetable oil
 2 teaspoons dry white wine
 1 teaspoon cornstarch
 1 teaspoon salt
 1 teaspoon finely chopped gingerroot
 1 teaspoon dark soy sauce
 1 teaspoon sesame oil
 ½ teaspoon sugar
 ¼ teaspoon white pepper

 8 medium dried black mushrooms
 ½ ounce tiger lily buds
 1 green onion (with top)

Remove bones and skin from chicken; cut chicken into strips, 2 × ½ inch. Toss chicken, vegetable oil, wine, cornstarch, salt, gingerroot, soy sauce, sesame oil, sugar and white pepper in glass or plastic bowl. Cover and refrigerate 1 hour.

Soak mushrooms in warm water until soft, about 30 minutes; drain. Rinse in warm water; drain. Remove and discard stems; cut caps into thin slices. Soak tiger lily buds in warm water until soft, about 5 minutes; drain. Remove and discard tips; cut buds lengthwise into halves. Cut green onion into 2-inch pieces.

Place chicken in 9-inch pie plate; stir in mushrooms and tiger lily buds. Place plate on rack in steamer; cover and steam over boiling water 20 minutes. (Add boiling water if necessary.) Garnish with green onion. *5 servings.*

Microwave Reheat Directions: Prepare Steamed Chicken with Black Mushrooms and Tiger Lily Buds as directed except — omit green onion; cover and refrigerate no longer than 24 hours. Just before serving, prepare green onion. Cover chicken mixture tightly and microwave on microwaveproof platter or bowl on high (100%) power 4 minutes; stir. Cover and microwave until hot, about 3 minutes longer. Garnish with green onion.

Curried Chicken

2 whole chicken breasts (about 2 pounds)
 1 egg white
 1 teaspoon cornstarch
 1 teaspoon salt
 1 teaspoon light soy sauce
 ¼ teaspoon white pepper

 2 medium tomatoes
 1 medium onion
 2 tablespoons cornstarch
 2 tablespoons cold water
 2 tablespoons dark soy sauce

 3 tablespoons vegetable oil
 1 cup frozen peas

 2 tablespoons vegetable oil
 1 teaspoon finely chopped gingerroot
 1 tablespoon curry powder
 ¼ cup chicken broth
 1 can (4 ounces) small button mushrooms, drained

Remove bones and skin from chicken; cut chicken into ¾-inch pieces. Mix egg white, 1 teaspoon cornstarch, the salt, 1 teaspoon soy sauce and the white pepper in glass or plastic bowl; stir in chicken. Cover and refrigerate 20 minutes.

Place tomatoes in boiling water 1 minute; plunge into cold water. Slip off skins. Cut tomatoes into ½-inch slices. Cut onion into 8 pieces. Mix 2 tablespoons cornstarch, the water and 2 tablespoons soy sauce.

Heat wok until 1 or 2 drops of water bubble and skitter when sprinkled in wok. Add 3 tablespoons vegetable oil; rotate wok to coat side. Add chicken and peas; stir-fry until chicken turns white. Remove chicken and peas from wok.

Add 2 tablespoons vegetable oil to wok; rotate. Add onion and gingerroot; stir-fry until gingerroot is light brown. Add tomatoes and curry powder; stir-fry 30 seconds. Add chicken and peas; stir-fry 1 minute. Stir in chicken broth; heat to boiling. Cover and boil 1 minute. Stir in mushrooms; cook 1 minute. Stir in cornstarch mixture; cook and stir until thickened, about 10 seconds. *5 servings.*

Chicken Almond Ding

2 whole chicken breasts (about 2 pounds)
1 egg white
1 teaspoon salt
1 teaspoon cornstarch
1 teaspoon soy sauce
 Dash of white pepper

2 medium carrots
2 tablespoons oyster sauce or 1 tablespoon dark
   soy sauce
1 tablespoon plus 1 teaspoon cornstarch
¼ teaspoon water

 Vegetable oil

2 tablespoons vegetable oil
¼ cup diced onion
1 teaspoon finely chopped garlic
1 teaspoon finely chopped gingerroot
1 cup diced celery
½ cup diced canned water chestnuts
1 teaspoon salt
½ cup diced bamboo shoots
1 can (4 ounces) button mushrooms, drained
½ cup chicken broth
1 cup frozen peas
½ cup roasted whole almonds
2 tablespoons chopped green onions (with tops)

Chicken Almond Ding

Remove bones and skin from chicken; cut chicken into ½-inch pieces. Mix egg white, 1 teaspoon salt, 1 teaspoon cornstarch, the soy sauce and white pepper in glass or plastic bowl; stir in chicken. Cover and refrigerate 30 minutes.

Cut carrots into ½-inch pieces. Place carrots in boiling water. Cover and cook 1 minute. Immediately rinse under running cold water; drain. Mix oyster sauce, 1 tablespoon plus 1 teaspoon cornstarch and the water.

Heat vegetable oil (1 inch) in wok to 325°. Add chicken; fry, turning frequently, until chicken turns white. Remove from wok to strainer. Wash and dry wok thoroughly.

Heat wok until 1 or 2 drops of water bubble and skitter when sprinkled in wok. Add 2 tablespoons vegetable oil; rotate wok to coat side. Add onion, garlic and gingerroot; stir-fry until garlic is light

brown. Add celery, water chestnuts and 1 teaspoon salt; stir-fry 1 minute. Add bamboo shoots and mushrooms; stir-fry 1 minute. Stir in carrots, chicken and chicken broth. Heat to boiling; cover and cook 2 minutes. Stir in cornstarch mixture; cook and stir until thickened, about 20 seconds. Stir in peas. Garnish with almonds and green onions. *6 servings.*

Microwave Reheat Directions: Prepare Chicken Almond Ding as directed except — omit peas, almonds and green onions; cover and refrigerate no longer than 24 hours. Just before serving, prepare peas, almonds and green onions. Cover chicken mixture tightly and microwave on microwaveproof platter or bowl on high (100%) power 5 minutes; stir in peas. Cover and microwave until hot, about 5 minutes longer. Garnish with almonds and green onions.

Cold Chicken and Fun See

Vegetable oil
2 ounces cellophane noodles (bean thread)

1 teaspoon vegetable oil
1 egg, slightly beaten
1 tablespoon sesame seed
3 cups shredded cooked chicken
1/2 head lettuce, shredded
1 carrot, shredded

3 tablespoons Hoisin sauce
2 tablespoons wine vinegar
2 teaspoons sugar
2 teaspoons soy sauce (light or dark)
2 teaspoons sesame oil

Heat vegetable oil (1 inch) in wok to 425°. Fry 1/4 of the noodles at a time until puffed, turning once, about 5 seconds. Drain on paper towel. Wash and dry wok thoroughly.

Heat wok until 1 or 2 drops of water bubble and skitter when sprinkled in wok. Add 1 teaspoon vegetable oil; rotate wok to coat side. Add egg; rotate wok to coat bottom with egg. Fry egg until firm, turning once, about 10 seconds. Remove egg from wok; cut into thin strips. Add sesame seed to wok; turn off heat. Cook and stir sesame seed until light brown. Drain on paper towel. Place chicken, lettuce, carrot and egg strips in large bowl; sprinkle with sesame seed.

Mix Hoisin sauce, vinegar, sugar, soy sauce and sesame oil. Pour sauce over meat and vegetables; add noodles. Toss before serving. 8 servings.

Do-ahead Tip: Fry cellophane noodles as directed. Store in airtight container at room temperature no longer than 5 days.

Cellophane noodles puff up to more than twice their original size when fried.

Kung Po Chicken

2 whole chicken breasts (about 2 pounds)
1 egg white
1 teaspoon cornstarch
1 teaspoon soy sauce (light or dark)
1/2 teaspoon salt
    Dash of white pepper
1 large green pepper
1 medium onion
1 tablespoon cornstarch
1 tablespoon cold water
1 tablespoon dry white wine
1/2 teaspoon sugar
1/4 teaspoon sesame oil

1/4 cup vegetable oil
1/2 cup skinned raw peanuts or unsalted
    roasted peanuts
1/8 teaspoon salt

1 clove garlic, crushed
1 teaspoon finely chopped gingerroot
2 tablespoons Hoisin sauce
2 teaspoons chili paste*
1/2 cup chicken broth

*1 teaspoon finely chopped dried chili pepper and 1 tablespoon soy sauce can be substituted for the chili paste.

Remove bones and skin from chicken; cut chicken into 3/4-inch pieces. Mix egg white, 1 teaspoon cornstarch, the soy sauce, 1/2 teaspoon salt and the white pepper in glass or plastic bowl; stir in chicken. Cover and refrigerate 30 minutes. Cut green pepper into 3/4-inch pieces. Cut onion into 8 pieces. Mix 1 tablespoon cornstarch, the water, wine, sugar and sesame oil.

Heat wok until 1 or 2 drops of water bubble and skitter when sprinkled in wok. Add 1/4 cup vegetable oil; rotate wok to coat side. Fry peanuts until light brown, about 30 seconds. Remove peanuts from wok; drain on paper towel. Sprinkle with 1/8 teaspoon salt.

Add onion, garlic and gingerroot to wok; stir-fry until onion is light brown, about 1 minute. Add chicken; stir-fry until chicken turns white. Add Hoisin sauce and chili paste; cook and stir 30 seconds. Stir in chicken broth; heat to boiling. Stir in cornstarch mixture; cook and stir until thickened. Add green pepper; cook and stir 30 seconds. Sprinkle with peanuts. 4 servings.

Chicken with Vegetables

2 whole chicken breasts (about 2 pounds)
1 egg white
1 teaspoon cornstarch
1 teaspoon salt
1 teaspoon light soy sauce
  Dash of white pepper

8 ounces bok choy (about 4 large stalks)
8 ounces pea pods
¼ cup cold water
2 tablespoons cornstarch
2 tablespoons oyster sauce
½ teaspoon sugar

3 tablespoons vegetable oil

3 tablespoons vegetable oil
1 teaspoon finely chopped gingerroot
2 cloves garlic, finely chopped
1 teaspoon salt
1 cup sliced mushrooms
½ cup sliced canned bamboo shoots
½ cup sliced canned water chestnuts
¾ cup chicken broth
2 teaspoons dry white wine

Remove bones and skin from chicken; cut chicken into ½-inch slices. Mix egg white, 1 teaspoon cornstarch, 1 teaspoon salt, the soy sauce and white pepper in glass or plastic bowl; stir in chicken. Cover and refrigerate 30 minutes.

Separate bok choy leaves from stems. Cut leaves into 2-inch pieces; cut stems into ¼-inch slices (do not combine leaves and stems). Remove strings from pea pods. Place pea pods in boiling water. Cover and cook 1 minute; drain. Rinse under running cold water; drain. Mix water, 2 tablespoons cornstarch, the oyster sauce and sugar.

Heat wok until 1 or 2 drops of water bubble and skitter. Add 3 tablespoons vegetable oil; rotate wok to coat side. Add chicken; stir-fry until chicken turns white. Remove chicken from wok.

Add 3 tablespoons vegetable oil; rotate to coat side. Add gingerroot and garlic; stir-fry until garlic is light brown. Add bok choy stems and 1 teaspoon salt; stir-fry 30 seconds. Add mushrooms, bamboo shoots and water chestnuts; stir-fry 1 minute. Stir in chicken, bok choy leaves, chicken broth and wine. Cover and cook 2 minutes. Stir in cornstarch mixture; cook and stir until thickened. Add pea pods; cook and stir 30 seconds. *6 servings.*

Chicken with Fun See

6 medium dried black mushrooms
2 whole chicken breasts (about 2 pounds)
1 egg white
1 teaspoon cornstarch
1 teaspoon salt
1 teaspoon light soy sauce
  Dash of white pepper

4 ounces cellophane noodles (bean thread)
4 ounces pea pods
2 green onions
1 tablespoon cornstarch
1 tablespoon cold water
1 tablespoon dark soy sauce
1 teaspoon sugar

⅓ cup vegetable oil
1 clove garlic, finely chopped
1 teaspoon finely chopped gingerroot

2 tablespoons vegetable oil
1½ cups thinly sliced celery cabbage
½ cup shredded canned bamboo shoots
1½ cups chicken broth

Soak mushrooms in warm water until soft, about 30 minutes; drain. Rinse in warm water; drain. Remove and discard stems; shred caps. Remove bones and skin from chicken; shred chicken (see page 52). Mix egg white, 1 teaspoon cornstarch, 1 teaspoon salt, 1 teaspoon soy sauce and the white pepper in glass or plastic bowl; stir in chicken. Cover and refrigerate 20 minutes.

Soak noodles in cold water 20 minutes; drain. Cut noodles into 3- to 4-inch pieces. Remove strings from pea pods. Place pea pods in boiling water. Cover and cook 1 minute; drain. Immediately rinse under running cold water; drain. Cut green onions into 2-inch pieces. Mix 1 tablespoon cornstarch, the water, 1 tablespoon soy sauce and the sugar.

Heat wok until 1 or 2 drops of water bubble and skitter. Add ⅓ cup vegetable oil; rotate wok to coat. Add chicken, garlic and gingerroot; stir-fry until chicken turns white. Remove chicken from wok.

Add 2 tablespoons vegetable oil; rotate to coat side. Add mushrooms, celery cabbage and bamboo shoots; stir-fry 1 minute. Stir in chicken and chicken broth; heat to boiling. Add noodles; heat to boiling. Stir in cornstarch mixture; cook and stir until thickened. Add pea pods; cook and stir 30 seconds. Garnish with green onions. *6 servings.*

Stir-fried Chicken with Bean Sprouts

6   *medium dried black mushrooms*
2   *whole chicken breasts (about 2 pounds)*
1   *egg white*
1   *teaspoon cornstarch*
1   *teaspoon salt*
1   *teaspoon light soy sauce*
    Dash of white pepper

1   *pound bean sprouts*
6   *green onions (with tops)*
1/4 *cup sugar*
1/4 *cup oyster sauce*
2   *tablespoons cornstarch*
2   *tablespoons cold water*

1/4 *cup vegetable oil*
1   *teaspoon finely chopped garlic*
1   *teaspoon grated gingerroot*

2   *tablespoons vegetable oil*
1/2 *cup chicken broth*

Soak mushrooms in warm water until soft, about 30 minutes; drain. Rinse in warm water; drain. Remove and discard stems; cut caps into thin slices. Remove bones and skin from chicken; cut chicken into strips, 2 × 1 inch. Mix egg white, 1 teaspoon cornstarch, the salt, soy sauce and white pepper in glass or plastic bowl; stir in chicken. Cover and refrigerate 20 minutes.

Rinse bean sprouts in cold water; drain. Cut green onions into 2-inch pieces; cut lengthwise into thin strips. Mix sugar, oyster sauce, 2 tablespoons cornstarch and the water.

Heat wok until 1 or 2 drops of water bubble and skitter when sprinkled in wok. Add 1/4 cup vegetable oil; rotate wok to coat side. Add chicken, garlic and gingerroot; stir-fry until chicken turns white. Remove chicken from wok.

Add 2 tablespoons vegetable oil to wok; rotate to coat side. Add mushrooms and bean sprouts; stir-fry 1 minute. Stir in chicken and chicken broth; heat to boiling. Stir in cornstarch mixture; cook and stir until thickened, about 30 seconds. Stir in green onions. *6 servings.*

Stir-fried Chicken with Mushrooms

2   *whole chicken breasts (about 2 pounds)*
1   *egg white*
1   *teaspoon cornstarch*
1   *teaspoon salt*
1   *teaspoon light soy sauce*
    Dash of white pepper

1   *pound mushrooms*
4   *ounces pea pods*
2   *tablespoons cornstarch*
2   *tablespoons cold water*

3   *tablespoons vegetable oil*
2   *cloves garlic, finely chopped*
1   *teaspoon finely chopped gingerroot*

2   *tablespoons vegetable oil*
1/2 *cup chicken broth*
1   *tablespoon oyster sauce*

Remove bones and skin from chicken; cut chicken into 1/4-inch slices. Mix egg white, 1 teaspoon cornstarch, 1 teaspoon salt, the soy sauce and white pepper in glass or plastic bowl; stir in chicken. Cover and refrigerate 30 minutes.

Cut mushrooms into 1/2-inch slices. Remove strings from pea pods. Place pea pods in boiling water. Cover and boil 1 minute; drain. Immediately rinse under running cold water; drain. Mix 2 tablespoons cornstarch and the water.

Heat wok until 1 or 2 drops of water bubble and skitter when sprinkled in wok. Add 3 tablespoons vegetable oil; rotate wok to coat side. Add chicken, garlic and gingerroot; stir-fry until chicken turns white. Remove chicken from wok.

Add 2 tablespoons vegetable oil to wok; rotate to coat side. Add mushrooms; stir-fry 1 minute. Stir in chicken and chicken broth; heat to boiling. Stir in cornstarch mixture; cook and stir until thickened, about 10 seconds. Add pea pods and oyster sauce; cook and stir 30 seconds. *6 servings.*

Microwave Reheat Directions: Prepare Stir-fried Chicken with Mushrooms; cover and refrigerate no longer than 24 hours. Cover tightly and microwave on microwaveproof platter or bowl on high (100%) power 4 minutes; stir. Cover and microwave until hot, 5 minutes longer.

Chicken with Cashews (Szechwan Style)

2   *whole chicken breasts (about 2 pounds)*
1   *egg white*
1   *teaspoon cornstarch*
1   *teaspoon soy sauce (light or dark)*
    Dash of white pepper
1   *large green pepper*
1   *medium onion*
1   *can (8½ ounces) sliced bamboo shoots, drained*
1   *tablespoon cornstarch*
1   *tablespoon cold water*
1   *tablespoon soy sauce (light or dark)*

2   *tablespoons vegetable oil*
1   *cup raw cashews*
¼   *teaspoon salt*

1   *teaspoon finely chopped gingerroot*
2   *tablespoons vegetable oil*
1   *tablespoon Hoisin sauce*
2   *teaspoons chili paste**
¼   *cup chicken broth*
2   *tablespoons chopped green onions (with tops)*

*1 teaspoon finely chopped dried chili pepper and 1 tablespoon soy sauce can be substituted for the chili paste.

Remove bones and skin from chicken; cut chicken into ¼-inch pieces. Mix egg white, 1 teaspoon cornstarch, 1 teaspoon soy sauce and the white pepper in glass or plastic bowl; stir in chicken. Cover and refrigerate 20 minutes. Cut green pepper into ¾-inch pieces. Cut onion into 8 pieces. Cut bamboo shoots into ½-inch pieces. Mix 1 tablespoon cornstarch, the water and 1 tablespoon soy sauce.

Heat wok until 1 or 2 drops of water bubble and skitter when sprinkled in wok. Add 2 tablespoons vegetable oil; rotate wok to coat side. Stir-fry cashews until light brown, about 1 minute. Remove cashews from wok; drain on paper towel. Sprinkle with salt. Add chicken to wok; stir-fry until chicken turns white. Remove chicken from wok.

Add onion pieces and gingerroot to wok; stir-fry until gingerroot is light brown. Stir in bamboo shoots. Add 2 tablespoons vegetable oil; rotate wok to coat side. Add chicken, green pepper, Hoisin sauce and chili paste; stir-fry 1 minute. Stir in chicken broth; heat to boiling. Stir in cornstarch mixture; cook and stir until thickened, about 20 seconds. Stir in cashews and green onions. *5 servings.*

Microwave Reheat Directions: Prepare Chicken with Cashews as directed except — omit green onions; cover and refrigerate no longer than 24 hours. Store fried cashews in airtight container at room temperature no longer than 24 hours. Just before serving, prepare green onions. Cover chicken mixture tightly and microwave on microwaveproof platter or bowl on high (100%) power 4 minutes; stir. Cover and microwave until hot, about 3 minutes longer. Stir in cashews and green onions. Cover and let stand 2 minutes.

Chicken Scrambled Eggs

1   whole chicken breast (about 1 pound)
½   teaspoon cornstarch
½   teaspoon salt

2   tablespoons vegetable oil
½   cup frozen peas

6   eggs, slightly beaten
¼   cup chopped green onions (with tops)
½   teaspoon salt
    Dash of white pepper

Remove bones and skin from chicken; cut chicken into ½-inch pieces. Toss chicken, cornstarch and ½ teaspoon salt.

Heat wok until 1 or 2 drops of water bubble and skitter when sprinkled in wok. Add 2 tablespoons vegetable oil; rotate wok to coat side. Add chicken; stir-fry until chicken turns white. Add peas; stir-fry 1 minute. Reduce heat to medium.

Mix eggs, green onions, ½ teaspoon salt and the white pepper; pour into wok. Cook and stir until eggs are thickened throughout but still moist, about 2 minutes. *4 servings.*

Wings with Oyster Sauce

8   chicken wings
2   green onions (with tops)

3   tablespoons vegetable oil
1   teaspoon finely chopped gingerroot
1   teaspoon finely chopped garlic
¼   cup oyster sauce
1   tablespoon dry white wine
1   teaspoon dark soy sauce
¾   cup chicken broth

1   tablespoon cornstarch
1   tablespoon cold water

Cut each chicken wing at joints to make 3 pieces; reserve tip to use in Chicken Broth (page 26). Cut green onions into 2-inch pieces.

Heat wok until 1 or 2 drops of water bubble and skitter. Add vegetable oil; rotate wok to coat. Add chicken, gingerroot and garlic; stir-fry 2 minutes.

Stir in oyster sauce, wine and soy sauce; stir to coat chicken. Stir in chicken broth; heat to boiling. Reduce heat; cover and simmer 15 minutes.

Mix cornstarch and water; stir into chicken mixture. Cook and stir until thickened, about 10 seconds. Garnish with green onions. *4 servings.*

Microwave Reheat Directions: Prepare Chicken Wings with Oyster Sauce as directed except — omit green onions; cover and refrigerate no longer than 24 hours. Just before serving, prepare green onions. Cover chicken mixture tightly and microwave on microwaveproof platter or bowl on high (100%) power 4 minutes; turn chicken. Cover and microwave until hot, about 3 minutes longer. Let stand covered 2 minutes. Garnish with green onions.

Wings with Black Beans

8   chicken wings
3   tablespoons salted black beans
2   green onions (with tops)

2   tablespoons vegetable oil
1   teaspoon finely shredded gingerroot
1   teaspoon finely chopped garlic
1   tablespoon dry white wine
2   teaspoons dark soy sauce
1   teaspoon sugar
¾   cup chicken broth

1   tablespoon cornstarch
1   tablespoon cold water

Cut each chicken wing at joints to make 3 pieces; reserve tip to use in Chicken Broth (page 26). Soak beans in warm water 15 minutes. Rinse in cold water to remove skins; drain. Mash beans. Cut green onions into 2-inch pieces.

Heat wok until 2 drops of water bubble and skitter. Add oil; rotate wok to coat. Add chicken, gingerroot and garlic; stir-fry 2 minutes. Add beans; stir-fry 1 minute. Stir in wine, soy sauce and sugar; stir to coat chicken. Stir in broth; heat to boiling. Reduce heat; cover and simmer 15 minutes.

Mix cornstarch and water; stir into chicken mixture. Cook and stir until thickened, about 10 seconds. Garnish with green onions. *4 servings.*

Peking Duck

$4\frac{1}{2}$ to 5-pound duckling
2 cloves garlic, crushed
1 tablespoon dry white wine
1 tablespoon soy sauce
1 teaspoon sugar
1 teaspoon salt
2 green onions (with tops)

6 cups water
$\frac{1}{2}$ cup honey
$\frac{1}{4}$ cup vinegar

4 green onion tops

$\frac{1}{2}$ cup Hoisin sauce

Fasten neck skin of duckling securely to back with skewers. Mix garlic, wine, soy sauce, sugar and salt. Place mixture and green onions in body cavity of duckling. Bring edges of tail opening together with skewers; tie tightly with heavy string. Insert needle of bicycle pump between skin and fat; pump air under skin until duckling is $1\frac{1}{2}$ times larger. (Do not let air escape. For crisp skin, it is necessary to separate skin from fat to release grease.)

Heat water and honey to boiling in wok; add vinegar. Tie 40-inch piece of heavy string to duckling legs. Hold duckling over wok. Pour water mixture over duckling for about 3 minutes. Hang duckling in refrigerator to dry at least 12 hours. Place pan under duckling to catch juices.

Place duckling breast side up on rack in shallow roasting pan. Roast uncovered in 400° oven 30 minutes. Turn duckling; roast 30 minutes longer. Reduce oven temperature to 375°. Turn duckling; roast until drumstick meat feels very soft, about 20 minutes longer. Let stand 15 minutes.

Cut green onion tops into 3-inch pieces; cut ¾-inch slits in each end. Chill in iced water until ends curl, about 10 minutes.

Remove skin and meat from bones; cut skin and meat into pieces, about 1½-inches. Arrange skin and meat on platter. Serve with Steamed Rolls (page 86) or Mandarin Pancakes (page 46). Brush Hoisin sauce on opened roll or pancake with green onion brush. Place green onion brush, skin and meat on roll or pancake; roll up. *8 servings.*

Peking Duck

Roast Duck

4½ to 5-pound duckling
1 tablespoon dry white wine
1 tablespoon soy sauce (light or dark)
1 teaspoon sugar
1 teaspoon salt
¼ teaspoon five spice powder
2 green onions (with tops)
2 cloves garlic

6 cups water
½ cup honey
¼ cup vinegar

2 green onions (with tops)

Fasten neck skin of duckling securely to back with skewers. Mix wine, soy sauce, sugar, salt and five spice powder. Place mixture, 2 green onions and the garlic in body cavity of duckling. Bring edges of tail opening together with skewers; tie tightly with heavy string.

Heat water and honey to boiling in wok; add vinegar. Tie 40-inch piece of heavy string to duckling legs. Hold duckling over wok. Pour water mixture over duckling for about 5 minutes. Hang duckling in refrigerator to dry at least 12 hours. Place pan under duckling to catch juices.

Place duckling breast side up on rack in shallow roasting pan. Roast uncovered in 400° oven 30 minutes. Turn duckling; roast 30 minutes longer. Reduce oven temperature to 350°. Turn duckling; roast until drumstick meat feels very soft, about 30 minutes. Let stand 15 minutes.

Cut 2 green onions into 2-inch pieces; cut several ¾-inch parallel slits in each end. Chill in iced water until ends curl, about 10 minutes.

Drain juices from duckling cavity; reserve. Remove meat; cut into pieces, 2 × 1 inch. Arrange meat on platter. Heat reserved juices to boiling; pour over meat. Garnish with green onions. *6 servings.*

Do-ahead Directions: Prepare Roast Duck as directed except — omit green onions for garnish; cover and refrigerate no longer than 24 hours. Cover and refrigerate reserved juices no longer than 24 hours. Just before serving, prepare green onions. Heat meat uncovered in ungreased square pan, 8 × 8 × 2 inches, in 400° oven until hot, 10 to 15 minutes. Heat reserved juices to boiling; pour over meat. Garnish with green onions.

Red Cooked Duck

12 medium dried black mushrooms
4 to 4½-pound duckling
1 tablespoon soy sauce (light or dark)
1 teaspoon sugar
1 teaspoon five spice powder

   Vegetable oil

2 tablespoons vegetable oil
4 thin slices gingerroot
2 cloves garlic, finely chopped
2 tablespoons dark soy sauce
2 cups chicken broth
1 teaspoon sugar

2 tablespoons cornstarch
2 tablespoons cold water

Soak mushrooms in warm water until soft, about 30 minutes; drain. Rinse in warm water; drain. Remove and discard stems; cut caps into ½-inch slices. Cut duckling into quarters; place in shallow glass dish. Mix 1 tablespoon soy sauce, 1 teaspoon sugar and the five spice powder; brush on duckling pieces. Cover and refrigerate 20 minutes. Wipe excess marinade from duckling; dry well.

Heat oil (1½ inches) in wok to 375°. Fry 2 duckling pieces at a time until golden brown, turning once, about 4 minutes. Drain on paper towel. Wash and dry wok thoroughly.

Heat wok until 1 or 2 drops of water bubble and skitter when sprinkled in wok. Add 2 tablespoons oil; rotate wok. Add gingerroot and garlic; stir-fry until garlic is light brown. Place duckling skin side down in wok. Add 2 tablespoons soy sauce; stir to coat duckling. Stir in mushrooms, chicken broth and 1 teaspoon sugar. Heat to boiling; reduce heat. Cover and simmer 1 hour. Remove duckling from wok; cool slightly. Remove bones and skin from duckling; cut meat into serving pieces.

Skim fat from broth; discard gingerroot. Heat broth to boiling. Mix cornstarch and water; stir into broth mixture. Cook and stir until thickened, about 10 seconds; pour over duckling. *6 servings.*

Do-ahead Directions: After cutting duckling into serving pieces, cover and refrigerate no longer than 24 hours. Prepare gravy; cover and refrigerate. Just before serving, heat duckling covered in 325° oven until hot, about 25 minutes. Heat gravy to boiling; pour over duckling.

Pressed Duck

4½ to 5-pound duckling
1 pound pork boneless loin or leg
½ cup sliced canned bamboo shoots
2 green onions

2 quarts water
½ cup soy sauce (light or dark)
4 thin slices gingerroot
3 cloves garlic, crushed
2 teaspoons salt
1 teaspoon five spice powder

⅓ cup sifted water chestnut flour
⅓ cup cornstarch
½ teaspoon salt
2 egg whites, slightly beaten

Vegetable oil
½ cup blanched almonds

1 cup chicken broth
¼ cup oyster sauce
3 tablespoons cornstarch
3 tablespoons cold water

Cut duckling lengthwise into halves. Trim fat from pork. Cut bamboo shoots into thin strips. Cut green onions into 2-inch pieces; cut pieces into thin strips.

Heat 2 quarts water, the soy sauce, gingerroot, garlic, 2 teaspoons salt and the five spice powder to boiling in 4-quart Dutch oven; add duckling and pork. Heat to boiling; reduce heat. Cover and simmer 1½ hours. Remove duckling and pork; cool. Skim fat from stock. Reserve and refrigerate 1 cup stock. Remove bones from duckling, keeping meat as whole as possible and leaving skin intact. Shred pork and any small duckling pieces.

Mix flour, ⅓ cup cornstarch and ½ teaspoon salt. Stir half of the flour mixture into shredded meat. Brush both sides of duckling pieces with half of the egg white. Sprinkle both sides with half of the remaining flour mixture. Place duckling skin side down in greased square pan, 9 × 9 × 2 inches. Press shredded meat firmly and evenly over duckling. Brush with remaining egg white; sprinkle with remaining flour mixture. Place pan on rack in steamer; cover and steam over boiling water 20 minutes. (Add boiling water if necessary.) Remove duckling from steamer; cover and refrigerate until cold, about 1 hour.

Heat vegetable oil (1½ inches) in wok to 350°. Fry almonds until light brown, about 1 minute. Remove from wok; drain on paper towel. Chop almonds finely. Fry one duckling piece at a time until golden brown, turning once, about 5 minutes. Drain on paper towel. Cut each piece lengthwise into halves; cut halves into ½-inch slices. Arrange on heated platter.

Heat reserved stock, the chicken broth, bamboo shoots and oyster sauce to boiling. Mix 3 tablespoons cornstarch and 3 tablespoons water; stir into stock mixture. Cook and stir until thickened; pour over duckling. Sprinkle with almonds; garnish with green onions. *8 servings.*

Do-ahead Directions: After steaming, cover duckling and reserved stock separately and refrigerate no longer than 24 hours. Just before serving, continue as directed.

Seafood

Sweet and Sour Shrimp

1 pound fresh or frozen raw shrimp
1 egg, slightly beaten
1 tablespoon cornstarch
1 teaspoon dry white wine
½ teaspoon light soy sauce
¼ teaspoon salt
1 medium carrot
1 small green pepper
2 tablespoons sesame seed

Vegetable oil
½ cup all-purpose flour
½ cup water
3 tablespoons cornstarch
1 tablespoon vegetable oil
½ teaspoon salt
½ teaspoon baking soda

1 cup sugar
cup chicken broth
⅓ cup white vinegar
1 tablespoon vegetable oil
2 teaspoons dark soy sauce
1 clove garlic, finely chopped
¼ cup cornstarch
¼ cup cold water
1 can (8¼ ounces) pineapple chunks, drained

Peel shrimp. (If shrimp is frozen, do not thaw; peel under running cold water.) Make a shallow cut lengthwise down back of each shrimp; wash out sand vein. Cut shrimp lengthwise into halves. Mix egg, 1 tablespoon cornstarch, the wine, ½ teaspoon soy sauce and ¼ teaspoon salt; stir in shrimp. Cover and refrigerate 10 minutes. Cut carrot diagonally into thin slices. Place carrot slices in boiling water. Cover and boil 1 minute; drain. Immediately rinse

under running cold water; drain. Cut green pepper into 1-inch pieces. Cook and stir sesame seed in 8-inch skillet over medium-high heat until light brown, about 2 minutes.

Heat vegetable oil (1½ inches) in wok to 350°. Mix flour, ½ cup water, 3 tablespoons cornstarch, 1 tablespoon vegetable oil, ½ teaspoon salt and the baking soda. Stir shrimp into batter until well coated. Fry 10 to 12 shrimp halves at a time until light brown, turning occasionally, 2 minutes. Drain on paper towel. Increase oil temperature to 375°. Fry shrimp all at one time until golden brown, about 1 minute. Drain on paper towel. Keep shrimp warm in 300° oven.

Heat sugar, chicken broth, vinegar, 1 tablespoon vegetable oil, 2 teaspoons soy sauce and the garlic to boiling in 2-quart saucepan. Mix ¼ cup cornstarch and ¼ cup water; stir into sauce. Cook and stir until thickened, about 10 seconds. Stir in carrot, green pepper and pineapple. Heat to boiling; pour over shrimp. Sprinkle with sesame seed. *6 servings.*

Do-ahead Directions: After frying shrimp 2 minutes, wrap, label and freeze no longer than 1 week. Prepare sauce as directed except — omit green pepper; freeze no longer than 1 week. Just before serving, prepare green pepper and sesame seed. Dip container of sauce into very hot water just to loosen. Place frozen block in 2-quart saucepan. Cover tightly; heat, stirring occasionally, until thawed. Place frozen shrimp on rack in jelly roll pan, 15½ × 10½ × 1 inch. Heat shrimp uncovered in 400° oven until hot, about 15 minutes. Stir green pepper into sauce. Heat to boiling; pour over shrimp. Sprinkle with sesame seed.

Sweet and Sour Shrimp

Sweet and Sour Fish

1¼ pounds walleye or cod fillets
1   egg
2   tablespoons cornstarch
1   tablespoon vegetable oil
½   teaspoon salt
3   thin slices gingerroot
¼   teaspoon sesame oil
⅛   teaspoon white pepper
2   small tomatoes
1   green pepper

    Vegetable oil
½   cup all-purpose flour
½   cup water
2   tablespoons cornstarch
½   teaspoon salt
½   teaspoon baking soda

1   cup sugar
1   cup chicken broth
¾   cup white vinegar
1   tablespoon vegetable oil
2   teaspoons dark soy sauce
½   teaspoon salt
1   clove garlic, finely chopped
¼   cup cornstarch
¼   cup cold water
1   can (8¼ ounces) pineapple chunks, drained

Remove skin from fish; cut across grain into ¾-inch pieces. Mix egg, 2 tablespoons cornstarch, 1 tablespoon vegetable oil, ½ teaspoon salt, the gingerroot, sesame oil and white pepper in glass bowl; stir in fish pieces. Cover and refrigerate 20 minutes; remove gingerroot. Cut each tomato into 8 wedges. Cut green pepper into ½-inch strips.

Heat vegetable oil (1½ inches) to 350°. Mix flour, ½ cup water, 2 tablespoons cornstarch, ½ teaspoon salt and the baking soda. Stir fish pieces into batter until coated. Fry about 10 pieces at a time until light brown, turning 2 or 3 times, about 3 minutes. Drain on paper towel. Increase oil temperature to 375°. Fry fish all at one time until golden brown, about 1 minute. Drain on paper towel.

Heat sugar, chicken broth, vinegar, 1 tablespoon vegetable oil, the soy sauce, ½ teaspoon salt and the garlic to boiling in 2-quart saucepan. Mix ¼ cup cornstarch and ¼ cup water; stir into sauce. Cook and stir until thickened, about 10 seconds. Stir in tomatoes, green pepper and pineapple. Heat to boiling; pour over fish. *8 servings.*

Sweet and Sour Whole Fish

2   drawn walleye or sea bass
        (1¼ pounds each)
1½ teaspoons salt
1½ teaspoons sesame oil
1   medium carrot
1   green pepper

    Vegetable oil
2   slices gingerroot
⅓   cup cornstarch

1   cup sugar
1   cup chicken broth or water
¾   cup white vinegar
1   tablespoon vegetable oil
2   teaspoons dark soy sauce
1   teaspoon salt
1   teaspoon finely chopped garlic
¼   cup cornstarch
¼   cup cold water
1   can (8¼ ounces) pineapple chunks, drained

Slash each fish crosswise 3 times on each side. Mix 1½ teaspoons salt and the sesame oil; rub cavities and outsides of fish with mixture. Cover and refrigerate 1 hour. Cut carrot diagonally into thin slices. Place carrot slices in boiling water. Cover and cook 1 minute; drain. Immediately rinse under running cold water; drain. Cut green pepper into ½-inch strips.

Heat vegetable oil (1 inch) in wok to 350°. Add gingerroot. Coat fish with ⅓ cup cornstarch. Fry one fish until golden brown, turning once, about 8 minutes. Keep fish warm in 300° oven. Repeat with remaining fish.

Heat sugar, chicken broth, vinegar, 1 tablespoon vegetable oil, the soy sauce, 1 teaspoon salt and the garlic to boiling in 2-quart saucepan. Mix ¼ cup cornstarch and the water; stir into sauce. Cook and stir until thickened, about 10 seconds. Stir in carrot, green pepper and pineapple. Heat to boiling; pour over fish. *4 servings.*

Sweet and Sour Scallops

3/4   pound scallops
2   tablespoons vegetable oil
1   teaspoon light soy sauce
1/4   teaspoon salt
1/4   teaspoon sesame oil
1/8   teaspoon white pepper
2   tomatoes
1   green pepper

      Vegetable oil
1/2   cup all-purpose flour
1/2   cup water
1/4   cup cornstarch
1   tablespoon vegetable oil
1   teaspoon baking soda
1/2   teaspoon salt

1   cup sugar
1   cup chicken broth or water
3/4   cup white vinegar
1   tablespoon vegetable oil
2   teaspoons dark soy sauce
1/2   teaspoon salt
1   clove garlic, finely chopped
1/4   cup cornstarch
1/4   cup cold water
1   can (8 1/4 ounces) pineapple chunks, drained

Toss scallops, 2 tablespoons vegetable oil, 1 teaspoon soy sauce, 1/4 teaspoon salt, the sesame oil and white pepper in glass or plastic bowl. Cover and refrigerate 20 minutes. Cut each tomato into 8 wedges. Cut green pepper into 1-inch pieces.

Heat vegetable oil (1 1/2 inches) in wok to 350°. Mix flour, 1/2 cup water, 1/4 cup cornstarch, 1 tablespoon oil, the baking soda and 1/2 teaspoon salt. Stir scallops into batter until well coated. Fry about 15 scallops at a time until light brown, turning occasionally, 2 minutes. Drain on paper towel. Increase oil temperature to 375°. Fry scallops all at one time until golden brown, about 1 minute. Drain on paper towel. Keep scallops warm in 300° oven.

Heat sugar, broth, vinegar, 1 tablespoon vegetable oil, 2 teaspoons soy sauce, 1/2 teaspoon salt and the garlic to boiling in 2-quart saucepan. Mix 1/4 cup cornstarch and 1/4 cup water; stir into sauce. Cook and stir until thickened, about 10 seconds. Stir in tomatoes, green pepper and pineapple. Heat to boiling; pour over scallops. *6 servings.*

Do-ahead Directions: After frying scallops 2 minutes, wrap, label and freeze no longer than 1 week. Prepare sauce as directed except — omit tomatoes and green pepper; freeze no longer than 1 week. Just before serving, prepare tomatoes and green pepper. Dip container of frozen sauce into very hot water just to loosen. Place frozen block in 2-quart saucepan. Cover tightly; heat, stirring occasionally, until thawed. Place frozen scallops on rack in jelly roll pan, 15 1/2 × 10 1/2 × 1 inch. Heat scallops uncovered in 400° oven until hot, about 15 minutes. Stir tomatoes and green pepper into sauce. Heat to boiling; pour over scallops.

Stir-fried Shrimp with Black Beans

1 pound fresh or frozen raw shrimp
1 teaspoon cornstarch
1 teaspoon dry white wine
1/4 teaspoon salt
1/4 teaspoon sesame oil
2 tablespoons salted black beans
1 tablespoon cornstarch
1/4 cup chicken broth
1 teaspoon dark soy sauce

1 tablespoon vegetable oil
1/2 pound ground pork

2 tablespoons vegetable oil
2 cloves garlic, finely chopped
1 teaspoon finely chopped gingerroot
1/4 cup chicken broth
2 tablespoons dry white wine
2 eggs, slightly beaten
2 green onions (with tops), chopped

Peel shrimp. (If shrimp is frozen, do not thaw; peel under running cold water.) Make a shallow cut lengthwise down back of each shrimp; wash out sand vein. Toss shrimp, 1 teaspoon cornstarch, 1 teaspoon wine, the salt and sesame oil in glass or plastic bowl. Cover and refrigerate 20 minutes. Soak beans in warm water 15 minutes; drain. Rinse beans in cold water to remove skins; drain. Mash beans. Mix 1 tablespoon cornstarch, 1/4 cup chicken broth and the soy sauce.

Heat wok until 1 or 2 drops of water bubble and skitter when sprinkled in wok. Add 1 tablespoon vegetable oil; rotate wok to coat side. Add pork; stir-fry until pork is no longer pink. Remove and drain. Wash and dry wok thoroughly.

Heat wok until 1 or 2 drops of water bubble and skitter when sprinkled in wok. Add 2 tablespoons vegetable oil; rotate wok to coat side. Add shrimp, mashed beans, garlic and gingerroot; stir-fry 1 minute. Stir in pork, 1/4 cup chicken broth and 2 tablespoons wine; heat to boiling. Stir in cornstarch mixture; heat to boiling. Stir in eggs. Remove from heat; cover and let stand 30 seconds. Sprinkle with green onions. *6 servings.*

Stir-fried Shrimp with Asparagus

10 medium dried black mushrooms
3/4 pound fresh or frozen raw shrimp
1/2 teaspoon cornstarch
1/2 teaspoon salt
1/4 teaspoon sesame oil
1/8 teaspoon white pepper

1 pound asparagus
4 ounces pea pods
2 green onions (with tops)
2 tablespoons cornstarch
2 tablespoons cold water

3 tablespoons vegetable oil
1 teaspoon finely chopped gingerroot
1 teaspoon finely chopped garlic

2 tablespoons vegetable oil
1 teaspoon salt
1/2 cup chicken broth
1 tablespoon oyster sauce

Soak mushrooms in warm water until soft, about 30 minutes; drain. Rinse in warm water; drain. Remove and discard stems; cut caps into 1/2-inch pieces. Peel shrimp. (If shrimp is frozen, do not thaw; peel under running cold water.) Make a shallow cut lengthwise down back of each shrimp; wash out sand vein. Cut shrimp lengthwise into halves. Toss shrimp, 1/2 teaspoon cornstarch, 1/2 teaspoon salt, the sesame oil and white pepper in glass or plastic bowl. Cover and refrigerate 10 minutes.

Break off tough ends of asparagus. Cut asparagus into 2-inch pieces. Remove strings from pea pods. Place pea pods in boiling water. Cover and cook 1 minute; drain. Immediately rinse under cold water; drain. Cut green onions into 2-inch pieces. Mix 2 tablespoons cornstarch and the water.

Heat wok until 2 drops of water bubble and skitter. Add 3 tablespoons vegetable oil; rotate wok. Add shrimp, gingerroot and garlic; stir-fry until shrimp is pink. Remove shrimp from wok.

Add 2 tablespoons vegetable oil to wok; rotate. Add mushrooms, asparagus and 1 teaspoon salt; stir-fry 2 minutes. Stir in chicken broth; heat to boiling. Stir in cornstarch mixture; cook and stir until thickened. Stir in shrimp, pea pods, green onions and oyster sauce; heat to boiling. *4 servings.*

Shrimp Subgum Wonton

½   *Fried Wonton recipe (page 18)*

¾   *pound fresh or frozen raw shrimp*
1   *teaspoon cornstarch*
¼   *teaspoon salt*
¼   *teaspoon sesame oil*
⅛   *teaspoon white pepper*

8   *ounces bok choy (about 4 large stalks)*
8   *ounces mushrooms*
6   *ounces pea pods*
¼   *cup oyster sauce*
2   *tablespoons cornstarch*
2   *tablespoons cold water*

3   *tablespoons vegetable oil*
½   *cup blanched almonds*
⅛   *teaspoon salt*
1   *large clove garlic, finely chopped*
1   *teaspoon finely chopped gingerroot*

3   *tablespoons vegetable oil*
1   *teaspoon salt*
½   *cup sliced canned bamboo shoots*
½   *cup canned water chestnuts, thinly sliced*
¾   *cup chicken broth*
1   *cup thinly sliced Barbecued Pork (page 14)*

Prepare 25 Fried Wontons as directed. Keep wontons warm in 300° oven. Wash and dry wok.

Peel shrimp. (If shrimp is frozen, do not thaw; peel under running cold water.) Make a shallow cut lengthwise down back of each shrimp; wash out sand vein. Cut shrimp lengthwise into halves. Toss shrimp, 1 teaspoon cornstarch, ¼ teaspoon salt, the sesame oil and white pepper in glass or plastic bowl. Cover and refrigerate 30 minutes.

Separate bok choy leaves from stems. Cut leaves into 2-inch pieces; cut stems diagonally into ¼-inch slices (do not combine leaves and stems). Cut mushrooms into ½-inch slices. Remove strings from pea pods. Place pea pods in boiling water. Cover and cook 1 minute; drain. Immediately rinse under running cold water; drain. Mix oyster sauce, 2 tablespoons cornstarch and the water.

Heat wok until 1 or 2 drops of water bubble and skitter when sprinkled in wok. Add 3 tablespoons vegetable oil; rotate wok to coat side. Add almonds; stir-fry until light brown, about 1 minute. Remove almonds from wok; drain on paper towel. Sprinkle

Shrimp Subgum Wonton

with ⅛ teaspoon salt. Add garlic and gingerroot to vegetable oil remaining in wok; stir-fry until light brown. Add shrimp; stir-fry until shrimp is pink. Remove shrimp from wok.

Add 3 tablespoons vegetable oil to wok; rotate to coat side. Add bok choy stems and 1 teaspoon salt; stir-fry 1 minute. Add bok choy leaves, mushrooms, bamboo shoots and water chestnuts; stir-fry 1 minute. Stir in chicken broth; heat to boiling. Stir in cornstarch mixture; cook and stir until thickened, about 10 seconds. Add shrimp; cook and stir 30 seconds. Stir in pea pods and pork. Arrange Fried Wontons around shrimp mixture; sprinkle with almonds. *8 servings.*

Shrimp Almond Ding

1   pound fresh or frozen raw shrimp
1   teaspoon cornstarch
1/2   teaspoon salt
1/2   teaspoon soy sauce
1/4   teaspoon sesame oil

3   stalks celery
1/2   cup sliced canned bamboo shoots
1/2   cup canned water chestnuts
1   medium onion
2   tablespoons cornstarch
2   tablespoons cold water

2   tablespoons vegetable oil
1/2   cup blanched almonds
1/8   teaspoon salt
1   teaspoon finely chopped garlic

2   tablespoons vegetable oil
1   teaspoon salt
1   can (4 ounces) button mushrooms, drained
1/2   cup chicken broth
1   tablespoon dry white wine
1/2   cup frozen peas
2   tablespoons oyster sauce
2   green onions (with tops), chopped

Peel shrimp. (If shrimp is frozen, do not thaw; peel under running cold water.) Make a shallow cut lengthwise down back of each shrimp; wash out sand vein. Cut shrimp lengthwise into halves. Toss shrimp, 1 teaspoon cornstarch, 1/2 teaspoon salt, the soy sauce and sesame oil in glass or plastic bowl. Cover and refrigerate 20 minutes.

Cut celery, bamboo shoots and water chestnuts into 1/2-inch pieces. Cut onion into 18 pieces. Mix 2 tablespoons cornstarch and the water.

Heat wok until 1 or 2 drops of water bubble and skitter when sprinkled in wok. Add 2 tablespoons vegetable oil; rotate wok to coat side. Add almonds; stir-fry until light brown, about 1 minute. Remove almonds from wok; drain on paper towel. Sprinkle with 1/8 teaspoon salt. Add onion pieces and garlic to wok; stir-fry until onion is tender. Add shrimp; stir-fry until shrimp is pink. Remove onion and shrimp from wok.

Add 2 tablespoons vegetable oil to wok; rotate to coat side. Add celery and 1 teaspoon salt; stir-fry 1 minute. Add bamboo shoots, water chestnuts and

mushrooms; stir-fry 1 minute. Stir in chicken broth and wine; heat to boiling. Stir in cornstarch mixture; cook and stir until thickened, about 10 seconds. Stir in shrimp, onion pieces, peas and oyster sauce; heat to boiling. Garnish with almonds and green onions. *5 servings.*

Microwave Reheat Directions: Prepare Shrimp Almond Ding as directed except — omit green onions; cover and refrigerate no longer than 24 hours. Store fried almonds in airtight container at room temperature no longer than 24 hours. Just before serving, prepare green onions. Cover shrimp mixture tightly and microwave on microwaveproof platter or bowl on high (100%) power 4 minutes; stir. Cover and microwave until hot, about 4 minutes longer. Let stand covered 2 minutes. Garnish with almonds and green onions.

Stir-fried Shrimp with Eggs

1/2   pound fresh or frozen raw shrimp
1   cup bean sprouts

3   tablespoons vegetable oil
1   teaspoon salt
6   eggs, slightly beaten
1/2   teaspoon salt
1/8   teaspoon white pepper
1/4   cup chopped green onions (with tops)
1/4   teaspoon sesame oil

Peel shrimp. (If shrimp is frozen, do not thaw; peel under running cold water.) Make a shallow cut lengthwise down back of each shrimp; wash out sand vein. Cut shrimp into 3/4-inch pieces. Rinse bean sprouts in cold water; drain.

Heat wok until 1 or 2 drops of water bubble and skitter when sprinkled in wok. Add vegetable oil; rotate wok to coat side. Add shrimp; stir-fry 1 minute. Add bean sprouts and 1 teaspoon salt; stir-fry 1 minute. Remove from wok to strainer. Mix eggs, 1/2 teaspoon salt and the white pepper. Add shrimp, bean sprouts, eggs, green onions and sesame oil to wok; cook and stir until eggs are thickened throughout but still moist. *4 servings.*

Stir-fried Shrimp with Vegetables

¾ pound fresh or frozen raw shrimp
½ teaspoon cornstarch
½ teaspoon light soy sauce
¼ teaspoon salt
⅛ teaspoon sesame oil
    Dash of white pepper

8 ounces bok choy (about 4 large stalks)
4 ounces pea pods
4 ounces mushrooms
2 green onions (with tops)
1 tablespoon cornstarch
1 tablespoon cold water

2 tablespoons vegetable oil
1 clove garlic, finely chopped
1 teaspoon finely chopped gingerroot

¼ cup vegetable oil
2 tablespoons oyster sauce or 1 tablespoon dark
    soy sauce
1 teaspoon salt
¼ cup chicken broth

Peel shrimp. (If shrimp is frozen, do not thaw; peel under running cold water.) Make a shallow cut lengthwise down back of shrimp; wash out sand vein. Cut shrimp lengthwise almost in half. Toss shrimp, ½ teaspoon cornstarch, the soy sauce, ¼ teaspoon salt, the sesame oil and pepper in glass or plastic bowl. Cover and refrigerate 30 minutes.

Separate bok choy leaves from stems. Cut leaves into 2-inch pieces; cut stems diagonally into ¼-inch slices (do not combine leaves and stems). Remove strings from pea pods. Place pea pods in boiling water. Cover and cook 1 minute; drain. Immediately rinse under running cold water; drain. Cut mushrooms into ½-inch slices. Cut green onions into 2-inch pieces. Mix 1 tablespoon cornstarch and the water.

Heat wok until 1 or 2 drops of water bubble and skitter when sprinkled in wok. Add 2 tablespoons vegetable oil; rotate wok to coat side. Add garlic and gingerroot; stir-fry until garlic is light brown. Add shrimp; stir-fry until shrimp is pink. Remove shrimp from wok.

Add ¼ cup vegetable oil to wok; rotate to coat side. Add bok choy stems and mushrooms; stir-fry 1 minute Stir in bok choy leaves, oyster sauce and 1 teaspoon salt. Stir in chicken broth; heat to boiling. Stir in cornstarch mixture; cook and stir until thickened, about 10 seconds. Add shrimp and pea pods; cook and stir 30 seconds. Garnish with green onions. *5 servings.*

Stir-fried Frog Legs

4 frog legs (about 1 pound)
1 teaspoon cornstarch
1 teaspoon finely chopped gingerroot
1 teaspoon light soy sauce
½ teaspoon salt
¼ teaspoon white pepper
¼ teaspoon sesame oil
6 ounces pea pods
2 green onions (with tops)
2 tablespoons cold water
1 tablespoon cornstarch
1 tablespoon soy sauce (light or dark)

2 tablespoons vegetable oil
1 teaspoon finely chopped gingerroot
1 teaspoon finely chopped garlic
1 can (8 ounces) straw mushrooms, drained
¼ cup chicken broth

Cut each frog leg at joints to make 3 pieces; discard tip. Cut thighs lengthwise into halves. Toss frog leg pieces, 1 teaspoon cornstarch, 1 teaspoon gingerroot, 1 teaspoon soy sauce, the salt, white pepper and sesame oil in glass or plastic bowl. Cover and refrigerate 20 minutes. Remove strings from pea pods. Place pea pods in boiling water. Cover and cook 1 minute; drain. Immediately rinse under running cold water; drain. Cut green onions into 2-inch pieces. Mix water, 1 tablespoon cornstarch and 1 tablespoon soy sauce.

Heat wok until 1 or 2 drops of water bubble and skitter when sprinkled in wok. Add vegetable oil; rotate wok to coat side. Add frog legs, 1 teaspoon gingerroot and the garlic; stir-fry 4 minutes. Stir in mushrooms and chicken broth; heat to boiling. Stir in cornstarch mixture; cook and stir until thickened, about 10 seconds. Add pea pods and green onions; cook and stir 1 minute. *6 servings.*

Stir-fried Fish with Vegetables

1	*pound walleye or sea bass fillets*
1½	*teaspoons vegetable oil*
1	*teaspoon cornstarch*
½	*teaspoon salt*
½	*teaspoon light soy sauce*
⅛	*teaspoon white pepper*
⅛	*teaspoon sesame oil*
1	*pound bok choy (about 7 large stalks)*
6	*ounces pea pods*
4	*ounces mushrooms*
2	*green onions (with tops)*
2	*tablespoons cornstarch*
2	*tablespoons cold water*
¼	*cup vegetable oil*
1	*teaspoon finely chopped gingerroot*
1	*teaspoon finely chopped garlic*
2	*tablespoons vegetable oil*
2	*tablespoons oyster sauce or 1 tablespoon dark soy sauce*
1	*teaspoon salt*
½	*cup chicken broth*

Cut fish across grain into ½-inch strips. Toss fish strips, 1½ teaspoons vegetable oil, 1 teaspoon corn- starch, ½ teaspoon salt, the soy sauce, white pepper and sesame oil in glass or plastic bowl. Cover and refrigerate 30 minutes.

Separate bok choy leaves from stems. Cut leaves into 2-inch pieces; cut stems diagonally into ¼-inch slices (do not combine leaves and stems). Remove strings from pea pods. Place pea pods in boiling water. Cover and cook 1 minute; drain. Im- mediately rinse under running cold water; drain. Cut mushrooms into ½-inch slices. Cut green on- ions into 2-inch pieces. Mix 2 tablespoons corn- starch and the water.

Heat wok until 1 or 2 drops of water bubble and skitter when sprinkled in wok. Add ¼ cup vege- table oil; rotate wok to coat side. Add gingerroot and garlic; stir-fry until light brown. Add fish; stir- fry until fish turns white. Remove fish from wok.

Add 2 tablespoons vegetable oil to wok; rotate to coat side. Add bok choy stems and mushrooms; stir-fry 1 minute. Stir in bok choy leaves, oyster sauce and 1 teaspoon salt. Stir in chicken broth; heat to boiling. Stir in cornstarch mixture; cook and stir until thickened. Add fish and pea pods; stir-fry 1 minute. Garnish with green onions. *6 servings.*

Stir-fried Fish
with Tomatoes

1	pound walleye or sea bass fillets
1	tablespoon vegetable oil
1	teaspoon cornstarch
1	teaspoon salt
1	teaspoon finely chopped gingerroot
1	teaspoon light soy sauce
1/4	teaspoon sesame oil
1/8	teaspoon white pepper
3	small tomatoes
2	green onions (with tops)
1	tablespoon cornstarch
1	tablespoon cold water
1/4	cup vegetable oil
1	small onion, thinly sliced
1	clove garlic, finely chopped
1	tablespoon dark soy sauce
1	tablespoon vegetable oil
1/4	cup chicken broth

Cut fish into strips, 2 × 1 inch. Toss fish strips, 1 tablespoon vegetable oil, 1 teaspoon cornstarch, the salt, gingerroot, 1 teaspoon soy sauce, the sesame oil and white pepper in glass or plastic bowl. Cover and refrigerate 30 minutes. Cut each tomato into 6 wedges. Cut green onions into 2-inch pieces. Mix 1 tablespoon cornstarch and the water.

Heat wok until 1 or 2 drops of water bubble and skitter when sprinkled in wok. Add 1/4 cup vegetable oil; rotate wok to coat side. Add onion slices and garlic; stir-fry until garlic is light brown. Add fish; stir-fry until fish turns white. Stir in 1 tablespoon soy sauce. Remove fish from wok.

Add 1 tablespoon vegetable oil to wok; rotate to coat side. Add tomatoes; stir-fry 30 seconds. Stir in chicken broth; heat to boiling. Stir in cornstarch mixture; cook and stir until thickened, about 30 seconds. Stir in fish and green onions. *4 servings.*

Stir-fried Fish
with Pea Pods

1	pound walleye or sea bass fillets
1	tablespoon vegetable oil
1	teaspoon cornstarch
1	teaspoon salt
1	teaspoon light soy sauce
1/4	teaspoon sesame oil
1/8	teaspoon white pepper
8	ounces pea pods
3	green onions (with tops)
3	tablespoons vegetable oil
1	clove garlic, finely chopped
1	teaspoon finely chopped gingerroot
2	tablespoons oyster sauce

Cut fish into strips, 2 × 1 inch. Toss fish strips, 1 tablespoon vegetable oil, the cornstarch, salt, soy sauce, sesame oil and white pepper in glass or plastic bowl. Cover and refrigerate 30 minutes. Remove strings from pea pods. Place pea pods in boiling water. Cover and cook 1 minute; drain. Immediately rinse under running cold water; drain. Cut green onions into 2-inch pieces.

Heat wok until 1 or 2 drops of water bubble and skitter when sprinkled in wok. Add 3 tablespoons vegetable oil; rotate wok to coat side. Add fish, garlic and gingerroot; stir-fry until fish turns white. Add pea pods and green onions; stir-fry 1 minute. Stir in oyster sauce. *4 servings.*

Shrimp-stuffed Black Mushrooms

Shrimp-stuffed Black Mushrooms

24   dried black mushrooms, 1½ inches
       in diameter
½   cup chicken broth
¼   pound fresh or frozen raw shrimp

2   ounces ground pork
1   tablespoon chopped green onion (with tops)
1   teaspoon cornstarch
½   teaspoon salt
⅛   teaspoon sesame oil
     Dash of white pepper

     Chicken broth
1   tablespoon dark soy sauce
2   teaspoons oyster sauce
⅛   teaspoon sesame oil
     Dash of white pepper
2   tablespoons cornstarch
2   tablespoons cold water
1   green onion (with top), chopped

Soak mushrooms in warm water until soft, about 30 minutes; drain. Rinse in warm water; drain. Remove and discard stems; soak caps in chicken broth 20 minutes. Drain mushroom caps; reserve chicken broth. Peel shrimp. (If shrimp is frozen, do not thaw; peel under running cold water.) Make a shallow cut lengthwise down back of each shrimp; wash out sand vein. Chop shrimp finely.

Mix shrimp, pork, 1 tablespoon green onion, 1 teaspoon cornstarch, the salt, ⅛ teaspoon sesame oil and dash of white pepper. Spread 1 teaspoon

shrimp mixture on stem side of each mushroom. Place mushrooms on heatproof plate. Place plate on rack in steamer; cover and steam over boiling water 20 minutes. (Add boiling water if necessary.)

Add enough chicken broth to reserved broth to measure 1½ cups. Heat chicken broth, soy sauce, oyster sauce, ⅛ teaspoon sesame oil and dash of white pepper to boiling. Mix 2 tablespoons cornstarch and the water; stir into broth mixture. Cook and stir until thickened, about 10 seconds. Pour sauce over mushrooms; garnish with chopped green onion. *6 servings.*

Do-ahead Directions: After spreading shrimp mixture on mushrooms, cover and refrigerate no longer than 24 hours. Prepare sauce as directed except — omit chopped green onion; cover and refrigerate no longer than 24 hours. Just before serving, steam mushrooms as directed. Chop green onion. Heat sauce to boiling; pour over mushrooms. Garnish with green onion.

Pan Fried Shrimp

1   pound medium shrimp (in shells)
1   tablespoon dry white wine
1   teaspoon soy sauce (light or dark)
2   green onions (with tops)

¼   cup vegetable oil
¼   cup catsup
1   tablespoon light soy sauce
2   cloves garlic, finely chopped
2   teaspoons finely chopped gingerroot

Remove legs and tail from each shrimp. Leaving shell intact ¼ inch at each end, cut shell lengthwise down back with scissors. Remove sand vein with wooden pick. Toss shrimp, wine and 1 teaspoon soy sauce in glass bowl. Cover and refrigerate 20 minutes. Cut green onions into 2-inch pieces.

Heat wok until 1 or 2 drops of water bubble and skitter when sprinkled in wok. Add vegetable oil; rotate wok to coat side. Place shrimp in single layer in wok (do not overlap). Fry shrimp until pink, turning once, about 4 minutes. Stir in catsup, 1 tablespoon soy sauce, the garlic and gingerroot; cover and cook 1½ minutes. Add green onions; cook and stir 30 seconds. *4 servings.*

Stuffed Shrimp

¾ *pound fresh or frozen raw medium shrimp*
  (in shells)
¼ *pound fresh or frozen raw shrimp*
2 *green onions (with tops)*

¼ *pound ground pork*
¼ *cup chopped green onions (with tops)*
2 *tablespoons finely chopped canned bamboo shoots*
2 *teaspoons cornstarch*
1 *teaspoon salt*
¼ *teaspoon sesame oil*
  Dash of white pepper

  Vegetable oil
½ *cup all-purpose flour*
⅓ *cup water*
¼ *cup cornstarch*
2 *egg whites*
1 *tablespoon vegetable oil*
1 *teaspoon salt*
½ *teaspoon baking soda*
⅛ *teaspoon white pepper*

½ *cup chicken broth*
¼ *cup white vinegar*
¼ *cup catsup*
1 *tablespoon vegetable oil*
2 *tablespoons sugar*
1 *tablespoon cornstarch*
1 *tablespoon cold water*

Remove shells from the ¾ pound shrimp, leaving tails intact. Make a shallow cut lengthwise down back of each shrimp; wash out sand vein. (1) Cut shrimp lengthwise almost in half. (2) Spread shrimp to open; drain on paper towel.

Peel the ¼ pound shrimp. (If shrimp is frozen, do not thaw; peel under running cold water.) Make a shallow cut lengthwise down back of each shrimp; wash out sand vein. Chop shrimp finely. Cut the 2 green onions into 2-inch pieces; cut several ¾-inch parallel slits in each end. Chill in iced water to curl ends, about 10 minutes.

Mix chopped shrimp, the pork, chopped green onions, bamboo shoots, 2 teaspoons cornstarch, 1 teaspoon salt, the sesame oil and dash of white pepper. Spread 1 tablespoon shrimp mixture on each shrimp. Place shrimp in oblong baking dish, 12 × 7½ × 2 inches.

Heat vegetable oil (1½ inches) in wok to 350°. Mix flour, ⅓ cup water, ¼ cup cornstarch, the egg whites, 1 tablespoon vegetable oil, 1 teaspoon salt, the baking soda and ⅛ teaspoon white pepper. Pour batter over shrimp; turn shrimp carefully until well coated. Fry 5 or 6 shrimp at a time until light brown, turning occasionally, 2 to 3 minutes. Drain on paper towel. Increase oil temperature to

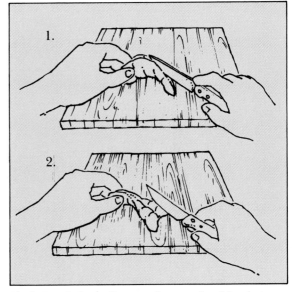

375°. Fry shrimp all at one time until golden brown, about 1 minute. Drain on paper towel. Keep shrimp warm in 300° oven.

Heat chicken broth, vinegar, catsup, 1 tablespoon vegetable oil and the sugar to boiling in 1-quart saucepan. Mix 1 tablespoon cornstarch and 1 tablespoon water; stir into broth mixture. Cook and stir until thickened, about 10 seconds. Pour sauce over shrimp; garnish with green onion pieces. *4 servings.*

Do-ahead Directions: Prepare Stuffed Shrimp as directed except — omit green onion pieces; wrap, label and freeze no longer than 1 month. Prepare sauce; cover and freeze no longer than 1 month. Just before serving, place frozen shrimp on rack in jelly roll pan, 15½ × 10½ × 1 inch. Heat uncovered in 425° oven until hot, about 20 minutes. Dip container of sauce into very hot water just to loosen. Place frozen block in 1-quart saucepan. Cover tightly; heat, stirring occasionally, until thawed. Prepare green onions. Heat sauce to boiling; pour over shrimp. Garnish with green onion pieces.

Shrimp Cakes
with White Radishes

½ pound fresh or frozen raw shrimp
¼ pound ground pork
6 canned water chestnuts, finely chopped
¼ cup finely chopped green onions (with tops)
1 teaspoon cornstarch
1 teaspoon salt
⅛ teaspoon sesame oil
   Dash of white pepper
1 pound white radishes
2 green onions (with tops)
1 tablespoon cornstarch
1 tablespoon cold water

2 tablespoons vegetable oil
1 tablespoon vegetable oil

2 tablespoons vegetable oil
2 cloves garlic, finely chopped
1 tablespoon dark soy sauce
½ teaspoon salt
½ cup chicken broth

Peel shrimp. (If shrimp is frozen, do not thaw; peel under running cold water.) Make a shallow cut lengthwise down back of each shrimp; wash out sand vein. Chop shrimp finely. Mix shrimp, pork, water chestnuts, ¼ cup green onions, 1 teaspoon cornstarch, 1 teaspoon salt, the sesame oil and white pepper. Cut radishes diagonally into ¼-inch slices. Cut 2 green onions into 2-inch pieces. Mix 1 tablespoon cornstarch and the water.

Heat wok until 1 or 2 drops of water bubble and skitter when sprinkled in wok. Add 2 tablespoons vegetable oil; rotate wok to coat side. Add half of the shrimp mixture; press and shape into large patty, ¼ inch thick and 7 inches in diameter. Fry patty until set, turning once, 4 to 6 minutes. Remove patty from wok; drain on paper towel. Add 1 tablespoon vegetable oil to wok; rotate to coat side. Repeat with remaining shrimp mixture. Cut patties into pieces, 1½ × 1 inch.

Add 2 tablespoons vegetable oil to wok; rotate to coat side. Add garlic; stir-fry until light brown. Add radishes; stir-fry 1 minute. Stir in soy sauce and ½ teaspoon salt. Stir in chicken broth; heat to boiling. Cover and cook 2 minutes. Stir in cornstarch mixture; cook and stir until thickened, about 10 seconds. Add shrimp pieces and green onions; cook and stir 1 minute. *5 servings.*

Do-ahead Directions: After frying Shrimp Cakes, wrap, label and freeze whole cakes no longer than 1 month. Just before serving, heat frozen cakes uncovered in 375° oven until hot, about 20 minutes. Cut cakes into pieces, 1½ × 1 inch. Prepare green onions and radish sauce. Continue as directed.

Abalone with
Mixed Vegetables

8 ounces bok choy (about 4 large stalks)
4 ounces pea pods
1 can (8 ounces) abalone, drained
1 can (8 ounces) baby corn, drained
2 green onions (with tops)
2 tablespoons oyster sauce
1 tablespoon cold water
1 teaspoon cornstarch
¼ teaspoon sesame oil

3 tablespoons vegetable oil
1 teaspoon finely chopped gingerroot
1 can (8 ounces) straw mushrooms, drained
1 teaspoon salt
½ cup chicken broth

Separate bok choy leaves from stems; discard leaves. Cut stems into ½-inch slices. Remove strings from pea pods. Place pea pods in boiling water. Cover and cook 1 minute; drain. Immediately rinse under running cold water; drain. Cut abalone into thin slices. Cut corn lengthwise into halves. Cut green onions into 2-inch pieces. Mix oyster sauce, water, cornstarch and sesame oil

Heat wok until 1 or 2 drops of water bubble and skitter when sprinkled in wok. Add vegetable oil; rotate wok to coat side. Add gingerroot; stir-fry until light brown. Add bok choy and corn; stir-fry 1 minute. Add mushrooms and salt; stir-fry 1 minute. Stir in chicken broth; heat to boiling. Stir in cornstarch mixture; cook and stir until thickened, about 10 seconds. Stir in pea pods, abalone and green onions; heat to boiling. *6 servings.*

Shrimp Egg Foo Yung

8   ounces bean sprouts
1   cup cooked shrimp
8   eggs, slightly beaten
1   jar (4½ ounces) sliced mushrooms, drained
2   green onions (with tops), chopped
½   teaspoon salt

3   tablespoons vegetable oil

1½ cups chicken broth
1   tablespoon dark soy sauce
1   teaspoon light soy sauce
¼   teaspoon salt
    Dash of white pepper
2   tablespoons cornstarch
2   tablespoons cold water

Rinse bean sprouts in cold water; drain. Cut shrimp into ½-inch pieces. Stir bean sprouts, shrimp, eggs, mushrooms, green onions and ½ teaspoon salt just to blend.

Heat wok until 1 or 2 drops of water bubble and skitter when sprinkled in wok. Add vegetable oil; rotate wok to coat side. Reduce heat to medium-high. Pour ½ cup egg mixture into wok. Push cooked egg up over shrimp with broad spatula to form patty. Fry patty until set and golden brown, turning once, about 4 minutes. Repeat with remaining egg mixture. (Add vegetable oil if necessary.) Keep patties warm in 300° oven.

Heat chicken broth, the soy sauces, ¼ teaspoon salt and the white pepper to boiling. Mix cornstarch and water; stir into broth mixture. Cook and stir until thickened, about 10 seconds; pour over patties. *6 servings.*

Note: For Pork Egg Foo Yung, substitute 1 cup ½-inch pieces Barbecued Pork (page 14) for the shrimp.

Do-ahead Directions: Fry egg patties; wrap, label and freeze no longer than 1 month. Just before serving, heat frozen patties uncovered in 375° oven until hot, about 25 minutes. Continue as directed.

Steamed Fish

1½ pound drawn walleye or sea bass
1   teaspoon finely chopped gingerroot
2   tablespoons vegetable oil
2   tablespoons brown bean sauce
2   cloves garlic, finely chopped
1   teaspoon salt
1   teaspoon soy sauce (light or dark)
¼   teaspoon sesame oil

2   green onions (with tops)

Slash fish crosswise 3 times on each side. Mix gingerroot, vegetable oil, bean sauce, garlic, salt, soy sauce and sesame oil; rub cavity and outside of fish with mixture. Cover and refrigerate 40 minutes.

Cut green onions into 2-inch pieces; cut pieces lengthwise into thin strips. Place fish on heatproof plate. Place plate on rack in steamer; cover and steam over boiling water until fish flakes easily with fork, about 15 minutes. (Add boiling water if necessary.) Garnish with green onions. *2 servings.*

Spinach-Egg Patties

1   package (10 ounces) frozen chopped spinach
6   eggs, slightly beaten
1   cup cooked small shrimp
¼   cup chopped green onions (with tops)
1   teaspoon salt
½   teaspoon sesame oil

3   tablespoons vegetable oil

Thaw spinach; drain. Mix spinach, eggs, shrimp, green onions, salt and sesame oil until blended.

Heat wok until 1 or 2 drops of water bubble and skitter. Add vegetable oil; rotate wok to coat. Reduce heat to medium-high. Pour ¼ cup egg mixture into wok. Fry patty until set and light brown, turning once, about 4 minutes. Keep patty warm in 300° oven. Repeat with remaining egg mixture. (Add vegetable oil if necessary.) Serve with soy sauce if desired. *6 servings.*

Rice, Noodles & Dumplings

Sizzling Rice with Shrimp

2	cups long grain white rice
2½	cups water
6	medium dried black mushrooms
1	whole chicken breast (about 1 pound)
1	egg white
½	teaspoon cornstarch
½	teaspoon salt
½	teaspoon light soy sauce
	Dash of white pepper
½	pound fresh or frozen raw shrimp
8	ounces bok choy (about 4 large stalks)
4	ounces pea pods
¼	cup oyster sauce
2	tablespoons cornstarch
2	tablespoons cold water
½	teaspoon sugar
½	teaspoon sesame oil
	Vegetable oil
3	tablespoons vegetable oil
1	large clove garlic, finely chopped
1	teaspoon finely chopped gingerroot
2	tablespoons vegetable oil
2	tablespoons dry white wine
1	teaspoon salt
½	cup sliced canned bamboo shoots
½	cup canned water chestnuts, thinly sliced
2	cups chicken broth

Place rice in 4-quart Dutch oven. Add enough cold water to cover rice. Wash rice by rubbing rice gently between fingers; drain. Repeat washing rice until water is clear, 5 or 6 times; drain. Add 2½ cups water; heat to boiling. Boil uncovered until almost all water has been absorbed. Cover and cook over low heat 30 minutes. Remove loose rice from pan; refrigerate for future use (to reheat, see page 80). Cook remaining rice uncovered over low heat until dry, about 1 hour. Break rice into 1½-inch pieces; place in single layer in ungreased oblong pan, 13×9×2 inches. Heat uncovered in 325° oven until dry, 20 minutes.

Soak mushrooms in warm water until soft; drain. Rinse in warm water; drain. Remove and discard stems; cut caps into ½-inch pieces. Remove bones and skin from chicken; cut into thin slices. Mix egg white, ½ teaspoon cornstarch, ½ teaspoon salt, the soy sauce and white pepper in glass bowl; stir in chicken. Cover and refrigerate 20 minutes.

Peel shrimp. Make a shallow cut lengthwise down back of each shrimp; wash out sand vein. Cut shrimp lengthwise into halves. Separate bok choy leaves from stems. Cut leaves into 2-inch pieces; cut stems diagonally into ¼-inch slices (do not combine leaves and stems). Remove strings from pea pods. Place pea pods in boiling water. Cover and cook 1 minute; drain. Immediately rinse under running cold water; drain. Mix oyster sauce, 2 tablespoons cornstarch, 2 tablespoons water, the sugar and sesame oil.

Heat vegetable oil (1 inch) in wok to 375°. Fry rice pieces until light brown, about 30 seconds. Drain on paper towel. Keep hot on heatproof platter in 300° oven. Add chicken to wok; stir-fry until white. Remove from wok to strainer. Wash and dry wok. Heat wok until 1 or 2 drops of water bubble and skitter. Add 3 tablespoons oil; rotate wok. Add shrimp, garlic and gingerroot; stir-fry until shrimp is pink; remove from wok.

Add 2 tablespoons oil to wok; rotate wok. Add bok choy stems, wine and 1 teaspoon salt; stir-fry 1 minute. Stir in mushrooms, bamboo shoots and water chestnuts. Stir in chicken broth; heat to boiling. Cover and cook 1 minute. Stir in chicken, shrimp and bok choy leaves; heat to boiling. Stir in cornstarch mixture; cook and stir until thickened. Add pea pods; cook and stir 30 seconds. Pour immediately over rice on heated platter. *8 servings.*

Note: Shrimp mixture must be very hot when poured over the hot rice — that's what makes the "sizzle."

White Rice

Place 2 cups long grain white rice in 2-quart saucepan. Add enough cold water to cover rice. Wash rice by rubbing rice gently between fingers; drain. Repeat washing rice until water is clear, 5 or 6 times; drain. Add 2 cups cold water; heat to boiling. Cover tightly; reduce heat and simmer until liquid is absorbed, 20 minutes. *6 cups.*

Do-ahead Directions: Prepare White Rice; cover tightly and refrigerate no longer than 5 days. Just before serving, place rice in heavy saucepan. Sprinkle water over rice, using about 2 tablespoons water to each 1 cup rice. Cover tightly; heat over low heat until hot, 5 to 8 minutes.

Stir-fried Rice

1	cup bean sprouts
1	tablespoon vegetable oil
2	eggs, slightly beaten
1	tablespoon vegetable oil
1	jar (2½ ounces) sliced mushrooms, drained
2	tablespoons vegetable oil
3	cups White Rice (above)
2	tablespoons dark soy sauce
	Dash of white pepper
1	cup cut-up cooked turkey, chicken, ham or Barbecued Pork (page 14)
2	green onions (with tops), chopped

Rinse bean sprouts in cold water; drain. Heat wok until 1 or 2 drops of water bubble and skitter when sprinkled in wok. Add 1 tablespoon vegetable oil; rotate wok to coat side. Add eggs; cook and stir until eggs are thickened throughout but still moist. Remove eggs from wok.

Add 1 tablespoon vegetable oil to wok; rotate to coat side. Add bean sprouts and mushrooms; stir-fry 1 minute. Remove from wok to strainer. Add 2 tablespoons vegetable oil to wok; rotate to coat side. Add rice; stir-fry 1 minute. Mix soy sauce and white pepper; stir into rice. Stir in turkey and green onions. Add bean sprouts, eggs and mushrooms; stir-fry 30 seconds. *4 servings.*

Microwave Reheat Directions: Prepare Stir-fried Rice; cover and refrigerate no longer than 24 hours. Cover tightly and microwave on microwaveproof platter or bowl on high (100%) power 4 minutes; stir. Cover and microwave until hot, about 3 minutes longer.

Chicken Fried Rice

1	whole chicken breast (about 1 pound)
½	teaspoon cornstarch
½	teaspoon salt
	Dash of white pepper
1	cup bean sprouts
1	tablespoon vegetable oil
2	eggs, slightly beaten
2	tablespoons vegetable oil
1	jar (2½ ounces) sliced mushrooms, drained
½	teaspoon salt
2	tablespoons vegetable oil
3	cups White Rice (opposite)
1	or 2 tablespoons dark soy sauce
	Dash of white pepper
2	green onions (with tops), chopped

Remove bones and skin from chicken; cut chicken into ¼-inch pieces. Toss chicken, cornstarch, ½ teaspoon salt and dash of white pepper. Rinse bean sprouts in cold water; drain.

Heat wok until 1 or 2 drops of water bubble and skitter when sprinkled in wok. Add 1 tablespoon vegetable oil; rotate wok to coat side. Add eggs; cook and stir until eggs are thickened throughout but still moist. Remove eggs from wok.

Add 2 tablespoons vegetable oil to wok; rotate to coat side. Add chicken; stir-fry until chicken turns white. Add bean sprouts, mushrooms and ½ teaspoon salt; stir-fry 1 minute. Remove from wok to strainer. Add 2 tablespoons vegetable oil to wok; rotate to coat side. Add rice; stir-fry 1 minute. Stir in soy sauce and dash of white pepper. Add chicken mixture, eggs and green onions; stir-fry 30 seconds. *5 servings.*

Microwave Reheat Directions: Prepare Chicken Fried Rice; cover and refrigerate no longer than 24 hours. Cover tightly and microwave on microwaveproof platter or bowl on high (100%) power 4 minutes; stir. Cover and microwave until hot, about 3 minutes longer.

Young Jewel Fried Rice

2   cups bean sprouts

2   tablespoons vegetable oil
3   eggs, slightly beaten

3   tablespoons vegetable oil
1   can (4 ounces) small button mushrooms, drained
1   teaspoon salt
3   tablespoons vegetable oil
4   cups White Rice (page 80)
3   tablespoons dark soy sauce
    Dash of white pepper
1   cup cooked shrimp
1   cup diced Barbecued Pork (page 14)
1/2   cup frozen peas
1/4   cup chopped green onions (with tops)

Rinse bean sprouts in cold water; drain.

Heat wok until 1 or 2 drops of water bubble and skitter when sprinkled in wok. Add 2 tablespoons vegetable oil; rotate wok to coat side. Add eggs; cook and stir until eggs are thickened throughout but still moist. Remove eggs from wok.

Add 3 tablespoons vegetable oil to wok; rotate to coat side. Add bean sprouts, mushrooms and salt; stir-fry 1 minute. Remove from wok to strainer. Add 3 tablespoons vegetable oil to wok; rotate to coat side. Add rice; stir-fry 1 minute. Mix soy sauce and white pepper; stir into rice. Stir in shrimp and pork. Add bean sprouts, mushrooms, eggs, peas and green onions; stir-fry 30 seconds. *7 servings.*

Microwave Reheat Directions: Prepare Young Jewel Fried Rice, cover and refrigerate no longer than 24 hours. Cover tightly and microwave on microwave-proof platter or bowl on high (100%) power 4 minutes; stir. Cover and microwave until hot, about 4 minutes longer.

MENU

Shrimp Toast, Barbecued Ribs
and Crabmeat Puffs

Sizzling Rice with Shrimp

Roast Duck

Young Jewel Fried Rice

Fried Rice Stick Noodles with Shrimp

1   pound fresh or frozen raw shrimp
1   teaspoon finely chopped gingerroot
1/2   teaspoon cornstarch
1/4   teaspoon salt
1/4   teaspoon sesame oil
    Dash of white pepper
1   pound celery cabbage
3   large green onions (with tops)
3   tablespoons cornstarch
3   tablespoons cold water
2   tablespoons dark soy sauce

    Vegetable oil
4   ounces rice stick noodles

2   tablespoons vegetable oil

2   tablespoons vegetable oil
1/2   cup shredded canned bamboo shoots
1   cup chicken broth

Peel shrimp. (If shrimp is frozen, do not thaw; peel under running cold water.) Make a shallow cut lengthwise down back of shrimp; wash out sand vein. Cut shrimp lengthwise into halves. Toss shrimp, gingerroot, 1/2 teaspoon cornstarch, the salt, sesame oil and white pepper. Cover and refrigerate 15 minutes. Cut celery cabbage into thin slices. Cut green onions into 2-inch pieces. Mix 3 tablespoons cornstarch, the water and soy sauce.

Heat vegetable oil (1 1/2 inches) in wok to 425°. Fry 1/4 of the noodles at a time until puffed and light brown, turning once, about 5 seconds. Drain on paper towel. Wash and dry wok thoroughly.

Heat wok until 1 or 2 drops of water bubble and skitter when sprinkled in wok. Add 2 tablespoons vegetable oil; rotate. Add shrimp; stir-fry until shrimp is pink. Remove shrimp from wok.

Add 2 tablespoons vegetable oil to wok; rotate to coat side. Add celery cabbage and bamboo shoots; stir-fry 2 minutes. Stir in chicken broth and shrimp; cover and heat to boiling. Stir in cornstarch mixture; cook and stir until thickened, about 10 seconds. Serve over noodles; garnish with green onions. *5 servings.*

Do-ahead Tip: Fry cellophane noodles as directed. Store in airtight container at room temperature no longer than 1 week.

Stir-fried Noodles and Beef

4	medium dried black mushrooms
1	pound beef boneless sirloin or round steak
1	tablespoon vegetable oil
1	teaspoon cornstarch
1/2	teaspoon light soy sauce
	Dash of white pepper
1	package (about 6 ounces) rice stick noodles

12	ounces bean sprouts
4	ounces pea pods
2	green onions (with tops)

3	tablespoons vegetable oil
1	teaspoon finely chopped gingerroot
1	teaspoon finely chopped garlic

2	tablespoons vegetable oil
1/4	cup shredded canned bamboo shoots
2	teaspoons chili paste*
1/2	teaspoon sugar
1 1/4	cups chicken broth
1	tablespoon soy sauce (light or dark)

*1 teaspoon finely chopped dried chili pepper mixed wth 1 tablespoon soy sauce can be substituted for the chili paste.

Soak mushrooms in warm water until soft, about 30 minutes; drain. Rinse in warm water; drain. Remove and discard stems; shred caps. Trim fat from beef; shred beef (see page 33). Toss beef, 1 tablespoon vegetable oil, 1 teaspoon cornstarch, 1/2 teaspoon soy sauce and the white pepper in glass or plastic bowl. Cover and refrigerate 20 minutes. Soak noodles in cold water 5 minutes; drain.

Rinse bean sprouts in cold water; drain. Remove strings from pea pods. Place pea pods in boiling water. Cover and cook 1 minute; drain. Immediately rinse under running cold water; drain. Cut pea pods lengthwise into 1/4-inch strips. Cut green onions into 2-inch pieces.

Heat wok until 1 or 2 drops of water bubble and skitter when sprinkled in wok. Add 3 tablespoons vegetable oil; rotate wok to coat side. Add beef, gingerroot and garlic; stir-fry until beef is brown, about 3 minutes. Remove beef from wok.

Add 2 tablespoons oil; rotate wok. Add mushrooms, sprouts, bamboo shoots, chili paste and sugar; stir-fry 1 minute. Stir in noodles, broth and soy sauce; heat to boiling. Cook and stir until noodles are tender, about 2 minutes. Stir in beef and pea pods; heat to boiling. Garnish with onions. *6 servings.*

Lo Mein

3/4	pound fresh or frozen raw shrimp
1	teaspoon cornstarch
1/2	teaspoon sesame oil
1/4	teaspoon salt
1/8	teaspoon white pepper

8	ounces bok choy (about 4 large stalks)
6	ounces pea pods
4	ounces mushrooms
2	green onions (with tops)
3	tablespoons cornstarch
3	tablespoons cold water

2	quarts water
1	package (8 ounces) Chinese egg noodles

2	tablespoons vegetable oil
1	teaspoon chopped gingerroot
1	teaspoon finely chopped garlic

2	tablespoons vegetable oil
1/4	cup oyster sauce
1	teaspoon salt
1	cup chicken broth
1	cup sliced Barbecued Pork (page 14)

Peel shrimp. (If shrimp is frozen, do not thaw; peel under running cold water.) Make shallow cut lengthwise down back of each shrimp; wash out sand vein. Cut shrimp lengthwise into halves. Toss shrimp, 1 teaspoon cornstarch, the sesame oil, 1/4 teaspoon salt and the white pepper in glass or plastic bowl. Cover and refrigerate 20 minutes.

Separate bok choy leaves from stems. Cut leaves into 2-inch pieces; cut stems diagonally into 1/4-inch slices (do not combine leaves and stems). Remove strings from pea pods. Place pea pods in boiling water. Cover and boil 1 minute; drain. Immediately rinse under running cold water; drain. Cut mushrooms in 1/2-inch slices. Cut green onions into 2-inch pieces. Mix 3 tablespoons cornstarch and 3 tablespoons water.

Heat 2 quarts water to boiling in Dutch oven. Stir in noodles. Cook uncovered over medium heat until noodles are soft and can be separated, about 5 minutes; drain. Keep noodles warm in 300° oven.

Heat wok until 1 or 2 drops of water bubble and skitter when sprinkled in wok. Add 2 tablespoons vegetable oil; rotate wok to coat side. Add shrimp, gingerroot and garlic; stir-fry until shrimp is pink. Remove shrimp from wok.

Add 2 tablespoons oil to wok; rotate to coat side. Add bok choy stems; stir-fry 1 minute. Add bok choy leaves, mushrooms, oyster sauce and 1 teaspoon salt; stir-fry 1 minute. Stir in chicken broth; heat to boiling. Stir in cornstarch mixture; cook and stir until thickened, about 10 seconds. Add shrimp, pea pods, green onions and Barbecued Pork; cook and stir 30 seconds. Serve over noodles. *6 servings.*

Cantonese Chow Mein

6   medium dried black mushrooms
1   pound beef boneless round steak
1   tablespoon vegetable oil
1   teaspoon salt
1   teaspoon cornstarch
1   teaspoon soy sauce (light or dark)
     Dash of white pepper

16   ounces bean sprouts
4   ounces pea pods
2   green onions (with tops)
2   tablespoons cornstarch
1/2 teaspoon sugar
2   tablespoons cold water

2   quarts water
1   package (8 ounces) Chinese egg noodles
1/4 cup vegetable oil

3   tablespoons vegetable oil
1   teaspoon finely chopped gingerroot
1   teaspoon finely chopped garlic

3   tablespoons vegetable oil
1/2 cup sliced canned bamboo shoots
1   teaspoon salt
1   cup chicken broth
2   tablespoons oyster sauce

Soak mushrooms in warm water until soft, about 30 minutes; drain. Rinse in warm water; drain. Remove and discard stems; cut caps into thin slices. Trim excess fat from beef; shred beef (see page 33). Toss beef, 1 tablespoon vegetable oil, 1 teaspoon salt, 1 teaspoon cornstarch, the soy sauce and white pepper in glass or plastic bowl. Cover and refrigerate 20 minutes.

Rinse bean sprouts in cold water; drain. Remove strings from pea pods. Place pea pods in boiling water. Cover and cook 1 minute; drain. Immediately rinse under running cold water; drain. Cut

green onions into 2-inch pieces. Mix 2 tablespoons cornstarch, the sugar and 2 tablespoons water.

Heat 2 quarts water to boiling in Dutch oven. Stir in noodles. Cook uncovered over medium heat until noodles are soft and can be separated, about 5 minutes; drain. Heat wok until 1 or 2 drops of water bubble and skitter when sprinkled in wok. Add 1/4 cup vegetable oil; rotate wok to coat side. Cook and stir noodles over medium heat until light brown. Keep noodles warm in 300° oven.

Add 3 tablespoons vegetable oil to wok; rotate to coat side. Add beef, gingerroot and garlic; stir-fry until beef is brown, about 3 minutes. Remove beef from wok.

Add 3 tablespoons vegetable oil to wok; rotate to coat side. Add mushrooms, bean sprouts, bamboo shoots and 1 teaspoon salt; stir-fry 1 minute. Stir in chicken broth and oyster sauce; heat to boiling. Stir in cornstarch mixture; cook and stir until thickened, about 10 seconds. Stir in beef and pea pods. Heat until beef is hot, about 1 minute. Serve over noodles; garnish with green onions. *8 servings.*

Cantonese Chow Mein

Pork Bou

1 cup milk
¼ cup sugar
1 tablespoon shortening
¼ teaspoon salt
1 package active dry yeast
2 tablespoons warm water (105 to 115°)
1 egg white
3 to 3½ cups all-purpose flour

6 medium dried black mushrooms
¾ pound pork boneless loin or leg
1 teaspoon cornstarch
1 teaspoon salt
½ teaspoon soy sauce (light or dark)
 Dash of white pepper
½ cup canned bamboo shoots
2 tablespoons oyster sauce
1 tablespoon cornstarch
1 tablespoon cold water

3 tablespoons vegetable oil
¼ cup chicken broth
3 green onions (with tops), finely chopped

Scald milk in 1-quart saucepan; stir in sugar, shortening and ¼ teaspoon salt until shortening is melted. Cool to lukewarm. Dissolve yeast in 2 tablespoons water. Stir yeast and egg white into milk mixture. Pour milk mixture over 3 cups of the flour in 2-quart bowl; stir until smooth. Mix in enough remaining flour to make dough easy to handle.

Turn dough onto lightly floured surface; knead until smooth and elastic, about 4 minutes. Place in greased bowl; turn greased side up. Cover; let rise in warm place until double, 1½ to 2 hours. (Dough is ready if indentation remains when touched.) Soak mushrooms in warm water until soft, about 30 minutes; drain. Rinse in warm water; drain. Remove and discard stems; cut caps into ¼-inch pieces. Cut pork into ¼-inch pieces. Toss pork, 1 teaspoon cornstarch, 1 teaspoon salt, the soy sauce and white pepper in glass or plastic bowl. Cover and refrigerate 20 minutes. Cut bamboo shoots into ¼-inch pieces. Mix oyster sauce, 1 tablespoon cornstarch and 1 tablespoon water.

Heat wok until 1 or 2 drops of water bubble and skitter when sprinkled in wok. Add vegetable oil; rotate wok to coat side. Add pork; stir-fry until no longer pink. Add mushrooms and bamboo shoots; stir-fry 1 minute. Stir in chicken broth; heat to boiling. Cover and cook 30 seconds. Stir in cornstarch mixture; cook and stir until thickened. Stir in green onions. Cover and refrigerate.

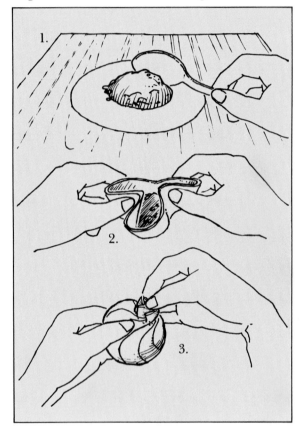

Punch down dough; divide into 20 pieces. Roll each piece into 3-inch circle. (1) Place 1 tablespoon pork mixture in center of circle. (2) Bring edge up around filling; (3) twist to seal. Place on 3-inch square of waxed paper. Repeat with remaining circles. Cover; let rise in warm place 20 minutes. Place Bou ½ inch apart on rack in steamer; cover and steam over boiling water 12 minutes. (Add boiling water if necessary.) Immediately remove waxed paper squares. *20 Bou.*

Do-ahead Directions: Prepare Pork Bou; cover and refrigerate no longer than 48 hours or wrap, label and freeze no longer than 2 months. To serve, place Bou on rack in steamer. Cover and steam 5 minutes if refrigerated, 30 minutes if frozen.

Barbecued Pork Bou

1   cup milk
¼   cup sugar
1   tablespoon shortening
¼   teaspoon salt
1   package active dry yeast
2   tablespoons warm water (105 to 115°)
1   egg white
3   to 3½ cups all-purpose flour

2   tablespoons vegetable oil
2   cups chopped Barbecued Pork (page 14)
2   tablespoons oyster sauce
½   cup chicken broth
1   tablespoon cornstarch
1   tablespoon cold water

Scald milk in 1-quart saucepan. Stir in sugar, shortening and salt until shortening is melted. Cool to lukewarm. Dissolve yeast in 2 tablespoons water. Stir yeast and egg white into milk mixture. Pour milk mixture over 3 cups of the flour in 2-quart bowl; stir until smooth. Mix in enough remaining flour to make dough easy to handle.

Turn dough onto lightly floured surface; knead until smooth and elastic, about 4 minutes. Place in greased bowl; turn greased side up. Cover; let rise in warm place until double, 1½ to 2 hours. (Dough is ready if indentation remains when touched.)

Heat wok until 1 or 2 drops of water bubble and skitter when sprinkled in wok. Add vegetable oil; rotate. Add Barbecued Pork; stir-fry 30 seconds. Stir in oyster sauce. Stir in chicken broth; heat to boiling. Mix cornstarch and 1 tablespoon water; stir into pork mixture. Cook and stir until thickened, about 10 seconds. Cover and refrigerate.

Punch down dough; divide into 20 pieces. Roll each piece into 3-inch circle. Place 1 tablespoon pork mixture in center of circle. Bring edge up around filling; twist to seal. (See illustrations on page 84.) Place on 3-inch square of waxed paper. Repeat with remaining circles. Cover; let rise in warm place 20 minutes. Place Bou ½ inch apart on rack in steamer; cover and steam over boiling water 12 minutes. (Add boiling water if necessary.) Remove waxed paper squares immediately. *20 Bou.*

Do-ahead Directions: Prepare Barbecued Pork Bou; cover and refrigerate no longer than 48 hours or wrap, label and freeze no longer than 2 months. Just before serving, steam refrigerated Bou 5 minutes, frozen Bou 30 minutes.

Pork Dumplings

8   to 10 medium dried black mushrooms
1   pound ground pork
½   cup finely chopped canned bamboo shoots
¼   cup finely chopped green onions (with tops)
1   egg white
2   tablespoons cornstarch
2   teaspoons salt
2   teaspoons light soy sauce
½   teaspoon sesame oil
¼   teaspoon white pepper

40 wonton skins
¼   cup light soy sauce
⅛   teaspoon sesame oil

Soak mushrooms in warm water until soft, about 30 minutes; drain. Rinse in warm water; drain. Remove and discard stems; chop caps finely. Mix mushrooms, pork, bamboo shoots, green onions, egg white, cornstarch, salt, 2 teaspoons soy sauce, ½ teaspoon sesame oil and the white pepper.

(1) Cut corners from wonton skins to make circles. (2) Place 1 tablespoon pork mixture in center of circle. (3) Bring edge up around filling, leaving top open. Repeat with remaining circles. Place dumplings in single layer on rack in steamer; cover and steam over boiling water 20 minutes. (Add boiling water if necessary.) Repeat with remaining dumplings. Mix ¼ cup soy sauce and ⅛ teaspoon sesame oil; serve with dumplings. *40 dumplings.*

Steamed Rolls

1   cup milk
¼   cup sugar
2   tablespoons shortening
¼   teaspoon salt
1   package active dry yeast
2   tablespoons warm water (105 to 115°)
1   egg white, slightly beaten
3¼ to 3½ cups all-purpose flour

    Sesame oil

Scald milk; stir in sugar, shortening and salt until shortening is melted. Cool to lukewarm. Dissolve yeast in water; let stand for 5 minutes. Stir yeast and egg white into milk mixture. Pour milk mixture over 3¼ cups of the flour; stir until smooth. Mix in enough flour to make dough easy to handle.

Turn dough onto lightly floured surface; knead until smooth and elastic, about 4 minutes. Place in greased bowl; turn greased side up. Cover; let rise in warm place until double, 1½ to 2 hours. (Dough is ready if indentation remains when touched.)

Punch down dough; divide into 20 pieces. Roll each piece into rectangle, 3 × 2 inches; brush with sesame oil. Roll up from narrow end. Place roll on 3-inch waxed paper square. Repeat with remaining pieces of dough. Cover; let rise in warm place 20 minutes. Place rolls in single layer ½ inch apart on rack in steamer; cover and steam over boiling water 8 minutes. (Add boiling water if necessary.) Repeat with remaining rolls. Remove waxed paper squares. Serve with Peking Duck (page 61) or as an accompaniment to a Chinese dinner. *20 rolls.*

Do-ahead Directions: Prepare Steamed Rolls; cover and refrigerate no longer than 48 hours or wrap, label and freeze no longer than 2 months. Just before serving, place rolls on rack in steamer. Cover and steam refrigerated rolls 5 minutes, frozen rolls 15 minutes.

Fried Dumplings

4   medium dried black mushrooms
1   pound ground pork
⅓   cup finely chopped canned bamboo shoots
¼   cup finely chopped green onions (with tops)
1   tablespoon dry white wine
1   tablespoon water
1   teaspoon cornstarch
1   teaspoon salt
1   teaspoon sesame oil
    Dash of white pepper

2   cups all-purpose flour
1   cup boiling water

½   cup vegetable oil
2   cups water
2   tablespoons soy sauce (light or dark)
1   teaspoon sesame oil

Soak mushrooms in warm water until soft, about 30 minutes; drain. Rinse in warm water; drain. Remove and discard stems; chop caps finely. Mix mushrooms, pork, bamboo shoots, green onions, wine, 1 tablespoon water, the cornstarch, salt, 1 teaspoon sesame oil and the white pepper.

Mix flour and 1 cup boiling water until a soft dough forms. Knead dough on lightly floured surface until smooth, about 5 minutes. Divide dough into halves. Shape each half into roll 12 inches long; cut each roll into ½-inch slices. Roll 1 slice of dough into a 3-inch circle. Place 1 teaspoon pork mixture on center of circle. Pinch 5 pleats on edge of one half of circle. Fold circle in half pressing pleated edge to unpleated edge. Repeat with remaining slices of dough.

Heat wok until 1 or 2 drops of water bubble and skitter when sprinkled in wok. Add 2 tablespoons of the vegetable oil; rotate wok to coat side. Place dumplings in single layer in wok; fry until bottoms are golden brown, about 2 minutes. Add ½ cup of the water. Cover and cook until water is absorbed, 6 to 7 minutes. Repeat with remaining dumplings. (Add vegetable oil as necessary.) Mix soy sauce and 1 teaspoon sesame oil; serve with dumplings. *48 dumplings.*

Shrimp Dumplings

Ginger-Soy Sauce (below)
½ pound fresh or frozen raw shrimp
1 cup water
2 ounces pork fat
¼ cup sliced canned bamboo shoots
1 tablespoon finely chopped green onions
  (with tops)
1 teaspoon vegetable oil
½ teaspoon cornstarch
½ teaspoon salt
⅛ teaspoon sesame oil
  Dash of white pepper

1¼ cups wheat starch
1 cup boiling water

Prepare Ginger-Soy Sauce. Peel shrimp. (If shrimp is frozen, do not thaw; peel under running cold water.) Make a shallow cut lengthwise down back of each shrimp; wash out sand vein. Cut shrimp into ½-inch pieces. Heat 1 cup water to boiling; add pork fat. Heat to boiling; cook uncovered 10 minutes. Drain. Cut bamboo shoots into ¼-inch pieces. Mix shrimp, pork fat, bamboo shoots, green onions, vegetable oil, cornstarch, salt, sesame oil and white pepper. Cover and refrigerate 10 minutes.

Mix wheat starch and 1 cup boiling water until a dough forms. Knead dough on lightly floured surface until smooth, about 3 minutes. Shape dough into roll 12 inches long; cut into ½-inch slices. Roll 1 slice of dough into a 3-inch circle. Place 1 teaspoon shrimp mixture in center of circle.

(1) Pinch 5 pleats on edge of one half of circle. (2) Fold circle in half pressing pleated edge to unpleat-ed edge. Repeat with remaining slices of dough. Place dumplings ¼ inch apart on heatproof plate. Place plate on rack in steamer; cover and steam over boiling water 10 minutes. (Add boiling water if necessary.) Serve with Ginger-Soy Sauce. *24 dumplings.*

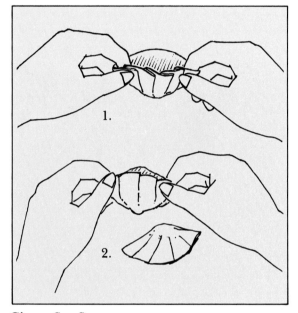

Ginger-Soy Sauce

¼ cup dark soy sauce
¼ cup white vinegar
2 teaspoons finely chopped gingerroot
2 teaspoons sesame oil
1 teaspoon finely chopped garlic

Mix all ingredients.

Vegetables

Stir-fried Hot and Sour Cabbage

1   medium head cabbage (about 1 pound)
3   green onions (with tops)
1   tablespoon cornstarch
1   tablespoon cold water

3   tablespoons vegetable oil
2   large cloves garlic, finely chopped
1/4   cup catsup
1   teaspoon salt
1   teaspoon red pepper sauce
1/2   cup chicken broth

Cut cabbage into 1½-inch pieces. Cut green onions into 2-inch pieces. Mix cornstarch and water.

Heat wok until 1 or 2 drops of water bubble and skitter when sprinkled in wok. Add vegetable oil; rotate wok to coat side. Add cabbage and garlic; stir-fry 1 minute. Add catsup, salt and pepper sauce; stir-fry 1 minute. Stir in chicken broth; heat to boiling. Stir in cornstarch mixture; cook and stir until thickened, about 10 seconds. Stir in green onions. *3 servings.*

Crispy Fried Carrots

4   medium carrots
4   green onions (with tops)

    Vegetable oil
3/4   cup water
1/4   cup all-purpose flour
3   tablespoons cornstarch
1   tablespoon vegetable oil
1   egg white
1/2   teaspoon salt
1/2   teaspoon baking soda

Shred carrots. Cut green onions into 3-inch pieces; cut pieces lengthwise into thin strips.

Heat vegetable oil (1½ inches) in 14-inch wok to 375°. (The oil will bubble up when the carrot mixture is added so be sure to use a large wok or Dutch oven.) Mix water, flour, cornstarch, 1 tablespoon vegetable oil, the egg white, salt and baking soda in 1½-quart bowl until smooth. (The batter will be very thin.) Stir carrots and green onions into batter. (Remove carrot mixture from batter with a slotted spoon.) Fry about half of the carrot mixture, turning frequently, until golden brown, about 1 minute. Drain on paper towel. Repeat with remaining carrot mixture. *3 servings.*

Zucchini and Mushrooms

1   pound zucchini
8   ounces mushrooms
1   tablespoon cornstarch
1   tablespoon cold water

1/4   cup vegetable oil
1   medium onion, thinly sliced
2   cloves garlic, finely chopped
1/2   teaspoon salt
2   tablespoons dark soy sauce
1/4   cup chicken broth

Cut zucchini lengthwise into halves; cut each half diagonally into ¼-inch slices. Cut mushrooms into ½-inch slices. Mix cornstarch and water.

Heat wok until 1 or 2 drops of water bubble and skitter when sprinkled in wok. Add vegetable oil; rotate wok to coat side. Add onion and garlic; stir-fry until garlic is light brown. Add zucchini, mushrooms and salt; stir-fry 2 minutes. Stir in soy sauce. Stir in chicken broth; heat to boiling. Stir in cornstarch mixture; cook and stir until thickened, about 10 seconds. *4 servings.*

Top to bottom: Zucchini and Mushrooms, Stir-fried Hot and Sour Cabbage, Crispy Fried Carrots

Stir-fried Bean Sprouts with Black Mushrooms

8   to 10 medium dried black mushrooms
1   pound bean sprouts
3   green onions (with tops)
1   tablespoon cornstarch
1   tablespoon cold water
1   tablespoon dark soy sauce

¼   cup vegetable oil
1   teaspoon finely chopped gingerroot
1   teaspoon salt
½   cup chicken broth

Soak mushrooms in warm water until soft, about 30 minutes; drain. Rinse in warm water; drain. Remove and discard stems; shred caps. Rinse bean sprouts in cold water; drain. Cut green onions into 2-inch pieces. Mix cornstarch, water and soy sauce.

Heat wok until 1 or 2 drops of water bubble and skitter when sprinkled in wok. Add vegetable oil; rotate wok to coat side. Add mushrooms, bean sprouts, gingerroot and salt; stir-fry 2 minutes. Stir in chicken broth; heat to boiling. Stir in cornstarch mixture; cook and stir until thickened, about 10 seconds. Stir in green onions. *3 servings.*

Asparagus with Black Mushrooms

8   to 10 medium dried black mushrooms
1   pound asparagus
4   ounces pea pods
2   green onions (with tops)
1   tablespoon cornstarch
1   tablespoon cold water

3   tablespoons vegetable oil
2   cloves garlic, crushed
½   teaspoon salt
1   tablespoon dark soy sauce
½   cup chicken broth

Soak mushrooms in warm water until soft, about 30 minutes; drain. Rinse in warm water; drain. Remove and discard stems; cut caps into ½-inch pieces. Break off tough ends of asparagus as far down as stalks snap easily. Cut asparagus into 2-inch pieces. Remove strings from pea pods. Place pea pods in boiling water. Cover and cook 1 minute; drain. Immediately rinse under running cold water; drain. Cut green onions into 2-inch pieces. Mix cornstarch and water.

Heat wok until 1 or 2 drops of water bubble and skitter when sprinkled in wok. Add vegetable oil; rotate wok to coat side. Add garlic; stir-fry until brown. Remove and discard garlic. Add mushrooms, asparagus and salt; stir-fry 1 minute. Stir in soy sauce. Stir in chicken broth; heat to boiling. Stir in cornstarch mixture; cook and stir until thickened, about 10 seconds. Add pea pods and green onions; cook and stir 30 seconds. *3 servings.*

Mixed Vegetables

8   ounces bok choy or celery (about 4 large stalks)
4   ounces pea pods
4   ounces mushrooms
2   green onions (with tops)
1   tablespoon cornstarch
1   tablespoon cold water

¼   cup vegetable oil
2   thin slices gingerroot, finely chopped
1   clove garlic, finely chopped
½   cup sliced canned bamboo shoots
½   cup chicken broth or water
1   teaspoon salt
2   tablespoons oyster sauce

Cut bok choy (with leaves) diagonally into ½-inch slices. Remove strings from pea pods. Place pea pods in boiling water. Cover and cook 1 minute; drain. Immediately rinse under running cold water; drain. Cut mushrooms into ¼-inch slices. Cut green onions into 2-inch pieces. Mix cornstarch and water.

Heat wok until 1 or 2 drops of water bubble and skitter when sprinkled in wok. Add vegetable oil; rotate wok to coat side. Add gingerroot and garlic; stir-fry until garlic is light brown. Add bok choy; stir-fry 1 minute. Add mushrooms and bamboo shoots; stir-fry 1 minute. Stir in chicken broth and salt; heat to boiling. Stir in cornstarch mixture; cook and stir until thickened, about 10 seconds. Add pea pods, green onions and oyster sauce; cook and stir 30 seconds. *3 servings.*

Stir-fried Shredded Carrots and Green Peppers

2   green onions (with tops)
1   medium green pepper
1   tablespoon cornstarch
1   tablespoon cold water

3   tablespoons vegetable oil
2   tablespoons shredded red chili pepper
1   tablespoon brown bean sauce
1   teaspoon finely chopped garlic
1   cup shredded carrots
1   can (8½ ounces) sliced bamboo shoots, drained
      and shredded
½   cup chicken broth
¼   teaspoon salt

Cut onions into 2-inch pieces. Cut green pepper into ¼-inch strips. Mix cornstarch and water.

Heat wok until 1 or 2 drops of water bubble and skitter when sprinkled in wok. Add vegetable oil; rotate wok to coat side. Stir in chili pepper, bean sauce and garlic. Add carrots and bamboo shoots; stir-fry 1 minute. Stir in chicken broth and salt; heat to boiling.

Stir in cornstarch mixture; cook and stir until thickened, about 10 seconds. Add onions and green pepper; cook and stir 30 seconds. *4 or 5 servings.*

Vegetable Cutting Techniques

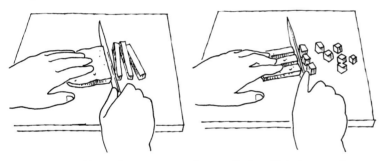

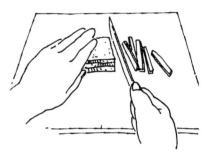

1. *Dicing or Cubing. Dice means to cut into small pieces ½ inch or smaller. Cube is to cut into pieces larger than ½ inch. Cut vegetables into strips ½ inch wide for dicing or larger for cubing. Stack or hold strips together and cut into pieces the same size as the width of the strips.*

2. *Shredding. Cut vegetables into ⅛-inch slices. Stack slices; cut into thin strips.*

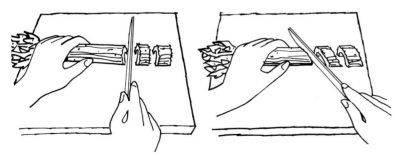

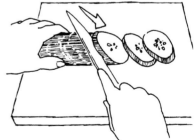

3. *Slicing Celery and Bok Choy. Cut straight across at the widest end of the stalk. As it becomes narrower, cut across the stalk at an angle.*

4. *Diagonal Slicing. Keep the blade angle of a very sharp knife almost parallel to the cutting surface to slice on the diagonal.*

Straw Mushrooms with Bean Curd

Straw Mushrooms
with Bean Curd

8	ounces bean curd
4	ounces pea pods
2	green onions (with tops)
1	tablespoon cornstarch
1	tablespoon cold water
3	tablespoons vegetable oil
4	thin slices gingerroot
1	can (8 ounces) whole straw mushrooms, drained
1/2	teaspoon salt
1/4	cup chicken broth
2	tablespoons oyster sauce or 1 tablespoon dark soy sauce

Cut bean curd into halves; cut each half into 1/4-inch slices. Remove strings from pea pods. Place pea pods in boiling water. Cover and cook 1 minute; drain. Immediately rinse under running cold water; drain. Cut green onions into 2-inch pieces. Mix cornstarch and water.

Heat wok until 1 or 2 drops of water bubble and skitter. Add vegetable oil; rotate wok to coat side. Add gingerroot; stir-fry until brown. Remove and discard gingerroot. Add bean curd; cook 20 seconds. Turn bean curd carefully; cook 20 seconds longer. Add mushrooms and salt; stir-fry 1 minute (do not break bean curd). Stir in chicken broth and oyster sauce; heat to boiling. Stir in corn-starch mixture; cook and stir until thickened, about 10 seconds. Add pea pods and green onions; cook and stir 30 seconds. *4 servings.*

Fun See Vegetables

6	medium dried black mushrooms
2	ounces cellophane noodles (bean thread)
1/2	ounce tiger lily buds
8	ounces celery cabbage or bok choy (about 4 large stalks)
4	ounces pea pods
4	ounces bean curd
2	green onions (with tops)
2	tablespoons vegetable oil
3	tablespoons vegetable oil
1	teaspoon finely chopped gingerroot
1	teaspoon salt
1/2	cup sliced canned bamboo shoots
1/2	cup sliced canned water chestnuts
1/2	cup water
2	tablespoons dark soy sauce
1/2	teaspoon sesame oil

Soak mushrooms in warm water until soft, about 30 minutes; drain. Rinse in warm water; drain. Remove and discard stems; cut caps into 1/2-inch pieces. Soak noodles in warm water 5 minutes; drain. Cut noodles into 4-inch pieces. Soak tiger lily buds in warm water until soft, about 5 minutes; drain. Remove and discard tips.

Cut celery cabbage into 1/2-inch slices. Remove strings from pea pods. Place pea pods in boiling water. Cover and cook 1 minute; drain. Immedi-ately rinse under running cold water; drain. Cut bean curd into halves; cut each half into 1/4-inch slices. Cut green onions into 2-inch pieces.

Heat wok until 1 or 2 drops of water bubble and skitter when sprinkled in wok. Add 2 tablespoons vegetable oil; rotate wok to coat side. Add bean curd; stir-fry carefully 1 minute. Remove bean curd from wok. Wash and dry wok thoroughly.

Heat wok until 1 or 2 drops of water bubble and skitter when sprinkled in wok. Add 3 tablespoons vegetable oil; rotate wok to coat side. Add mush-rooms, tiger lily buds, celery cabbage, gingerroot and salt; stir-fry 1 minute. Add bamboo shoots and water chestnuts; stir-fry 1 minute.

Stir in water; heat to boiling. Add noodles and pea pods; cook and stir 30 seconds. Add bean curd, green onions and soy sauce; cook and stir 30 seconds. Stir in sesame oil. *5 servings.*

Subgum Bean Curd

1   pound bean curd
8   ounces bok choy (about 4 large stalks)
4   ounces pea pods
1   medium red pepper
2   green onions (with tops)
2   tablespoons cornstarch
2   tablespoons cold water

3   tablespoons vegetable oil

2   tablespoons vegetable oil
1   can (8 ounces) whole straw mushrooms, drained
1/2 cup sliced canned water chestnuts
1/2 cup chicken broth
1/4 cup oyster sauce

Cut bean curd into pieces, 1 × 1 × 1/4 inch. Cut bok choy (with leaves) diagonally into 1/4-inch slices. Remove strings from pea pods. Place pea pods in boiling water. Cover and cook 1 minute; drain. Immediately rinse under running cold water; drain. Cut red pepper into 1/2-inch strips. Cut onions into 2-inch pieces. Mix cornstarch and water.

Heat wok until 1 or 2 drops of water bubble and skitter when sprinkled in wok. Add 3 tablespoons vegetable oil; rotate wok to coat side. Add bean curd; cook, stirring carefully, 2 minutes. Remove bean curd from wok.

Add 2 tablespoons vegetable oil to wok; rotate to coat side. Add bok choy; stir-fry 1 minute. Add mushrooms and water chestnuts; stir-fry 1 minute. Stir in chicken broth and oyster sauce; heat to boiling. Stir in cornstarch mixture; cook and stir until thickened. Stir in bean curd, red pepper, green onions and pea pods. *5 servings.*

Stir-fried Spinach

1   pound spinach
1/4 cup vegetable oil
1   teaspoon finely chopped garlic
1/4 cup chicken broth
1   teaspoon salt

Tear spinach into bite-size pieces. Heat wok until 1 or 2 drops of water bubble and skitter when sprinkled in wok. Add vegetable oil; rotate wok to coat side. Add garlic; stir-fry until light brown. Add spinach; stir-fry 2 minutes. Stir in chicken broth and salt. Cover and cook 1 minute. *2 servings.*

INDEX

SIMPLY THE BEST
GARNISH SET RECIPES

MARIAN GETZ

INTRODUCTION BY WOLFGANG PUCK

A most sincere thank you to our wonderful viewers and customers for without you there would be no need for a cookbook. I try very hard to give you an array of recipes suited for the particular kitchen tool the cookbook is written for. Wolfgang and I create recipes faster than we can write them down. That is what chefs do and is also the reason to tune in to the live shows and even record them so you can learn new dishes that may not be in our cookbooks yet.

Thank you most of all to Wolfgang. You are the most passionate chef I know and it has been a privilege to work for you since 1998. You are a great leader and friend. Your restaurants are full of cooks and staff that have been with you for 20 or more years which is a true testament to how you lead us. Thanks for allowing me to write these cookbooks and for letting me share the stage at HSN with you.

To Greg, my sweet husband since 1983. Working together is a dream and I love you. You have taught me what a treasure it is to have a home filled with laughter.

To my boys, Jordan and Ben, we have a beautiful life, don't we? And it just keeps on getting better since we added Lindsay, J.J. as well as precious grandbabies Easton, Sadie and Theodore.

To all the great people at WP Productions, Syd, Arnie, Mike, Phoebe, Michael, Nicolle, Tracy, Genevieve, Gina, Nancy, Sylvain and the rest of the team, you are all amazing to work with. Watching all the wonderful items we sell develop from idea to final product on live television is an awe-inspiring process to see and I love that I get to be a part of it.

To Daniel Koren, our patient editor and photographer, thank you for your dedication. You make the photo shoot days fun and you are such an easygoing person to work with in the cramped, hot studio we have to share. We have learned so much together and have far more to learn.

To Greg, Cat, Laurie, Martha, Maria, René, Jordan and Margarita who are the most dedicated, loving staff anyone could wish for. You are the true heroes behind the scenes. You are a well-oiled machine of very hard working people who pull off the live shows at HSN. It is a magical production to watch, from the first box unpacked, to the thousands of eggs cracked and beaten to running to get that "thing" Wolf asks for at the last minute, to the very last dish washed and put away it is quite a sight to behold. I love you all and I deeply love what we do.

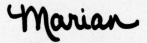

It is often said that you eat with your eyes first. Whether in my restaurants or at home, I believe that food presentation is a big part of how we experience our meals. The garnishing set will empower you to be more adventurous in the kitchen. Not only will you be able to prepare your food quicker, but also give it a decorative touch that will turn a great dish into an extraordinary experience.

When I asked Marian to write the cookbook for the garnishing set, I knew she would rise to the occasion. Her experience as a pastry chef, wife, mother, and now a grandmother allowed Marian to put together a garnishing cookbook with a wide variety of recipes that I'm sure you will use for years to come.

A student of cooking is probably one of the best ways to describe Marian. She is always looking for something new, something fresh, something local, something seasonal. Her culinary knowledge combined with her passion for cooking is second to none. The recipes that Marian has written for this cookbook will motivate you to be more creative in the kitchen.

As I learned long ago, alongside my mother and grandmother, you should always put lots of love into everything you cook. This is certainly evident in this cookbook.

Wolfgang Puck

INTRODUCTION BY WOLFGANG PUCK

3

TABLE OF CONTENTS

TABLE OF CONTENTS

GARNISHING TIPS

Your Wolfgang Puck Garnishing Set is a fantastic set of tools that gives you the ability to turn your home cooked dishes into beautiful restaurant-style presentations with ease. This cookbook will show you how to create decorative accents as well as elaborate fruit displays that will not only impress your friends and family but also spark your creativity by showing you how to create foods that look as amazing as they taste. Here is a more detailed explanation of each tool and how to best use it:

FRUIT AND VEGETABLE SCOOP

Scoop, deseed, hollow out and remove flesh for a variety of produce. The scoop quickly and easily removes flesh and seeds from fruits and vegetables like papaya, cantaloupe and squash. The scoop can also be used to separate melon, avocados, etc. from their skin. Even use to hollow out tomatoes or peppers. To use, hold handle and slide metal blade through the produce. Adjust the width of the blade by squeezing the handle.

LEVER SCOOP

This multi-purpose 1 tablespoon scoop molds perfectly shaped meatballs, evenly portioned scoops of tuna/chicken salad, ice cream, cookie dough, melon balls and much more. The pop up lever neatly and easily releases food with a simple push. To use, insert scoop and rotate. Push down on the lever to release.

SMALL AND LARGE CORERS

These two versatile size corers lend themselves to endless prep tasks and dishes. Use the small size to core apples, pears and jalapeño peppers. Get creative and use the corer to remove the center of cupcakes and then fill with your favorite filling or frosting. The large corer is ideal for removing the center of larger fruits and vegetables to make stuffed peppers, eggplant or tomatoes. Even use to cut fun coin sandwiches for kids or decorative round shaped butter.

To use, insert the cutting edge into your desired food and twist. Carefully remove the contents from the center of the corer.

CORN ZIPPER

Cleanly and effortlessly zip corn kernels from the cob. Safer than using a knife; the fine serrated teeth cut precisely between the kernels and the cob, removing several rows at once. Enhance dishes like corn chowder, creamed corn and corn fritter by using fresh corn from the cob.

To use, place corn horizontally on a cutting board and pull the zipper lengthwise across the kernels in one continuous motion. This tool be used to remove kernels from both raw and cooked corn.

VEGETABLE CURLER

This simple-to-use tool creates thin ribbons from hard vegetables such as carrots, cucumbers, squash and zucchini. Perfect for slicing vegetables for stir-fry, making ribbon salad or edible flowers and other decorative garnishes.

To use, cut the stem/end from your desired vegetable (straight, firm vegetables produce the best results). If you are using a root vegetable also peel the skin. Insert the end of vegetable into the opening of the curler. In one continuous motion turn the vegetable in the direction of the blade, similar to sharpening a pencil.

SANTOKU SHEARS

These all-purpose cutting shears feature an oversized blade that can tackle almost any household or kitchen task from snipping herbs or trimming fat from poultry to cutting flower stems. The shears also detach for easy cleaning and use as a knife.

To detach, fully open the shears and carefully pull the blades apart. To reattach, align the bolt and hole on the blades and carefully push the shears into the closed position.

CRINKLE CHOPPER

This unique tool produces uniform crinkle patterns when slicing food, while the large surface area allows you to easily transfer ingredients to your cookware or prep bowl. Ideal for making homemade French fries, crinkle potato chips, decorative cheese and crudité platters, etc.

To use, simply hold the chopper by the rolled handle and cut food to your desired size. The underside can be used as a shovel to scoop and transfer food.

TWIN CURL CUTTER

This unique gadget can turn ordinary food into fun, creative masterpieces. Create thick spiral curls from a variety of hard produce. Perfect for making homemade curly fries, vegetable candy canes or beautiful carrot curls for your salad. The cutter can also be used to remove the center from fruits and vegetables which can then be filled with your favorite filling.

To use, attach the handle to the shaft of the cutter, insert the pointed end into your desired fruit/ vegetable then turn the cutter in a clockwise direction until the curl blades cut through the opposite end. Remove the handle and slide the shaft through the end of your fruit/vegetable. Remove the cut curls by turning clockwise. To separate the curls simply twist them and turn in opposite directions.

WIDE BLADE PEELER

Trims the skin from a variety of produce with precision and ease. The wide blade design allows you to easily remove strips of skin from large root vegetables, butternut squash, eggplant and more. The right side of the peeler features a pointed end to remove eyes and blemishes from potatoes.

To use, place your fruit or vegetable horizontally on a cutting board and pull the peeler lengthwise across the produce.

8-BLADE SLICER

Cuts green onions, pickles, strawberries, mushrooms and other small fruits and vegetable into small uniform slices. Also, ideal for scoring mangos for easy removal from its skin.

To use, simply glide the slicer through your fruit/vegetable in one smooth motion. Replace protective cover after use.

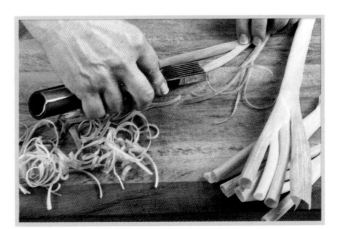

WATERMELON GELATIN
WEDGES

Makes 6-8 servings

Ingredients:

1 small watermelon
3 boxes (3 ounces each) watermelon flavored gelatin
1/2 of a honeydew melon
1/2 of a cantaloupe

Method:

1. *Using the SANTOKU KNIFE, cut the watermelon in half.*
2. *Using the FRUIT AND VEGETABLE SCOOP, remove melon flesh then transfer to a blender, liquefy and strain if necessary; reserve juice and discard pulp.*
3. *Prepare gelatin as instructed on the packaging using the watermelon juice instead of water.*
4. *Allow gelatin mixture to cool slightly.*
5. *Using the LEVER SCOOP, make balls from honeydew and cantaloupe then place in watermelon halves.*
6. *Place watermelon halves on a sheet pan in the refrigerator and verify that they are level. If necessary, use a coiled ring of aluminum foil under each melon and press until they are level.*
7. *Carefully pour gelatin mixture into watermelon halves to the top (you may have extra gelatin).*
8. *Refrigerate for a minimum of 4 hours or overnight until firm.*
9. *Using the SANTOKU KNIFE, slice watermelon into wedges and serve.*

SPRING VEGETABLE
RICOTTA PIE

Makes 8 servings

Ingredients:

1 package (14.1 ounces) refrigerated pie crust
1 carrot
1 zucchini
1 yellow squash
1 small yellow onion
5 asparagus spears

1 cup whole milk ricotta cheese
1 cup Parmesan cheese, grated
1/2 cup Swiss cheese, grated
1 cup whole milk
6 large eggs
Kosher salt and fresh pepper to taste

Method:

1. *Preheat oven to 400°F.*
2. *Unroll the pie crust over a 9-inch pie pan.*
3. *Using the WIDE BLADE PEELER, peel the carrot.*
4. *Using the VEGETABLE CURLER, make long spirals from the zucchini, squash and carrot.*
5. *Place these spirals in the pie pan evenly.*
6. *Using the SANTOKU KNIFE, slice the onion and chop the asparagus then add to the pie.*
7. *In a mixing bowl, whisk together remaining ingredients then pour into pie.*
8. *Bake on lower oven rack for 35-40 minutes or until well browned and puffed.*
9. *Remove, let cool for 10 minutes, garnish as desired and serve.*

TOMATO CREAM CHEESE TULIPS

Makes 9 servings

Ingredients:

9 Roma tomatoes
1 tub (8 ounces) chive flavored cream cheese, softened
1 bunch green onions
1 bunch leeks

Method:

1. *Using the SANTOKU KNIFE, cut a 1 1/2-inch deep "X" into each tomato opposite the stem end (figure 1).*
2. *Using the SMALL CORER, remove the stem end from each tomato (figure 2).*
3. *Using the LEVER SCOOP, make balls from the cream cheese.*
4. *Pry open the "X" in the tomatoes and press the cream cheese balls into the opening (figure 3).*
5. *Lay tomatoes on a serving tray.*
6. *Using the SANTOKU SHEARS, trim the green onions and remove the white parts.*
7. *Insert a green onion as the tulip's "stem" into the cored opening of each tomato (figure 4).*
8. *Using the SANTOKU SHEARS, cut the green part of the leeks into long, pointed leaf shapes.*
9. *Tie "tulips" together with a green onion then trim any loose ends using the SANTOKU SHEARS.*
10. *Serve as desired.*

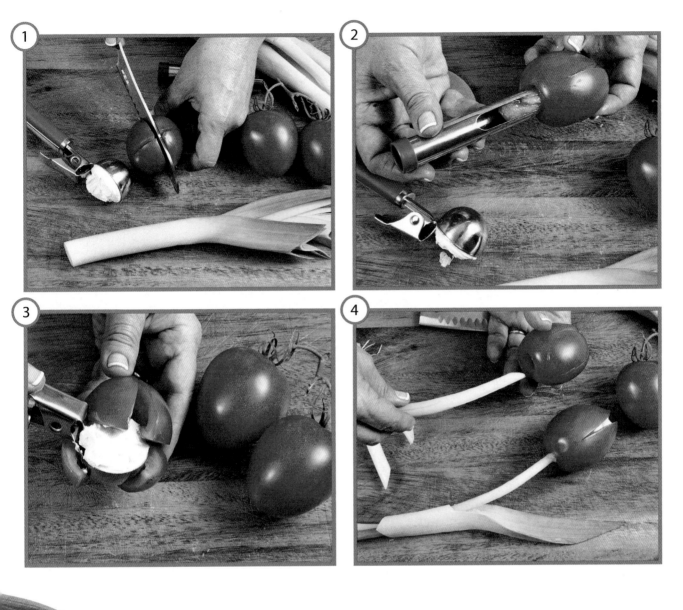

PINEAPPLE PECAN DIP

Makes 8-10 servings

Ingredients:

1 ripe pineapple

3 packages (8 ounces each) cream cheese, softened

1 1/2 cups powdered sugar

Zest and juice of one lemon

2 cups (about 120) toasted pecan halves

Assorted crackers or cookies for serving

Method:

1. *Using the SANTOKU KNIFE, cut off the top of the pineapple crown then cut it in half lengthwise; set pineapple crown aside.*

2. *Using the SANTOKU KNIFE, cut pineapple in half lengthwise then use the FRUIT AND VEGETABLE SCOOP to remove the pineapple flesh avoiding the tough core.*

3. *Discard pineapple shell then finely dice up the flesh using the SANTOKU KNIFE.*

4. *Place diced up flesh in a strainer and squeeze out as much juice as possible (save juice for another use or discard).*

5. *Stir together the cream cheese, powdered sugar, lemon zest, lemon juice and squeezed pineapple flesh until combined.*

6. *On a serving tray, spread the pineapple mixture into an oval shape then place pineapple crown at one end of the oval.*

7. *Press pecan halves onto oval starting just below the pineapple crown then work in rows until covered with pecan halves.*

8. *Using the SANTOKU SHEARS, trim pineapple crown if it is too large and serve.*

SPIRAL
FRENCH FRIES

Makes 2-4 servings

Ingredients:

3 cups canola oil
5 Russet potatoes
Kosher salt
Ketchup for serving

Method:

1. *Heat oil in a deep pot over medium heat until 300°F on a thermometer.*
2. *Using the TWIN CURL CUTTER, twist out spirals from the potatoes.*
3. *Rinse spirals in cool water then carefully but thoroughly pat dry.*
4. *When oil has reached 300°F, add potato spirals and fry for 8-10 minutes to soften (potatoes will be pale).*
5. *Remove and drain potatoes.*
6. *Increase stovetop temperature to medium-high until oil reaches 350°F then carefully add half of the potato spirals and fry for 2-3 minutes or until golden brown.*
7. *Remove, drain and season with salt immediately.*
8. *Repeat with remaining spirals and serve with ketchup.*

SPOOKY
POT PIE

Makes 4 servings

Ingredients:

2 teaspoons olive oil
1 bunch green onions
1 pound lean ground beef
2 teaspoons jarred beef bouillon base or to taste
Fresh pepper to taste
2 ears fresh corn
1 cup frozen peas
1 carrot
1 tube (16.3 ounces) refrigerated biscuits
4 black olives

RECIPES

Method:

1. *Preheat oven to 350°F and preheat the oil in a large skillet over medium heat.*
2. *Using the SANTOKU KNIFE, chop the green onions.*
3. *Place onions and beef into the skillet and stir to break up the beef.*
4. *Add bouillon and pepper then stir until beef is no longer pink.*
5. *Using the CORN ZIPPER, remove corn kernels into the skillet, add the peas and stir well.*
6. *Using the WIDE BLADE PEELER, peel the carrot then twist through the VEGETABLE CURLER, snip carrot curls into 2-inch lengths using the SANTOKU SHEARS then add to skillet and stir.*
7. *Remove from heat and divide between 4 oven-safe serving bowls.*
8. *Pat out biscuits on the counter into thin circles to make the spider's "body."*
9. *Pat out additional biscuits then use the SANTOKU KNIFE to cut into strips to make the spider's "legs".*
10. *Drape 8 strips from center outward over the lip of each bowl then place a cut out thin biscuit circle in the center of each bowl.*
11. *Using the SANTOKU KNIFE, slice olives then place 2 olive rings on each center to make the spider's "eyes".*
12. *Transfer bowls to a sheet pan and bake for 20 minutes or until light brown.*
13. *Remove and let slightly cool before serving.*

SPICED CIDER PUMPKIN KEG

Makes 8-10 servings

Ingredients:

1 large pumpkin or squash
1 keg spout (see source page 108)
1 orange
3 cinnamon sticks

10 whole cloves
8 cups apple cider
Spiced rum to taste (optional)
1/3 cup dark brown sugar

Method:

1. *Using the SANTOKU KNIFE, cut a thin piece from the bottom of the pumpkin so that it sits flat.*
2. *Using the SANTOKU KNIFE, cut off the pumpkin top and set top aside.*
3. *Using the FRUIT AND VEGETABLE SCOOP, remove the seeds and strings from the pumpkin.*
4. *Using the SMALL CORER, cut a hole into the side of the pumpkin for the keg spout. Adjust the hole size using the SANTOKU KNIFE if needed until spout fits tightly.*
5. *Using the WIDE BLADE PEELER, remove peel from the orange.*
6. *Place orange, cinnamon sticks and cloves on a cheesecloth square then tie into a bundle.*
7. *In a bowl, whisk together the cider, rum and sugar.*
8. *Add the spice bag to the bowl then refrigerate for a minimum of 3 hours or overnight.*
9. *When ready to serve, discard spice bag and pour into the pumpkin.*

TIP

Elevate keg 3-4 inches above counter to facilitate filling cups with cider.

PEAR & GRAPE
HEDGEHOG

Makes 1 serving

Ingredients:

1 pear
1 cup green grapes
1 black grape
2 whole cloves
Wooden picks for skewering

Method:

1. *Use the SANTOKU SHEARS to snip off the pear stem (figure 1).*
2. *Using the WIDE BLADE PEELER, peel the pear (figure 2).*
3. *Using the SANTOKU KNIFE, remove a slice of pear so that the pear sits flat horizontally.*
4. *Using the SANTOKU KNIFE, slice the black grape in half crosswise then attach 1 piece at the end of the pear to make the hedgehog's "nose" using a wooden pick to secure it (figure 3).*
5. *Insert the cloves into the pear to make the hedgehog's "eyes."*
6. *Skewer each grape leaving part of the wooden picks poking out of each end.*
7. *Arrange grapes along the pear, leaving the stem/neck of the pear area empty (figure 4).*
8. *Serve as desired.*

NOTE

Use caution when serving foods to small children that contain skewers or wooden picks.

NO BAKE CHOCOLATE
MERINGUE TARTS

Makes 3 servings

For the Crust:
2 cups chocolate sandwich cookies
6 tablespoons unsalted butter, melted

For the Filling:
2 cups semisweet chocolate chips
3/4 cup heavy cream

For the Topping:
3 large egg whites
1/4 cup granulated sugar
1/8 teaspoon cream of tartar
Piece of chocolate bar for shaving (optional)

Method:

1. *Using the SANTOKU KNIFE, finely chop the cookies until rough crumbs are achieved.*
2. *In a mixing bowl, combine cookie crumbs and butter then press into three 4-inch tart pans; set aside.*
3. *In a microwave-safe bowl, combine all filling ingredients, microwave for 2 minutes, stirring periodically until chocolate is melted and smooth then pour into tart pans and chill for 1 hour.*
4. *In a clean bowl, use a hand mixer on medium speed to combine the egg whites, sugar and cream of tartar until stiff peaks form.*
5. *Dip the LEVER SCOOP in hot water, shake off excess then scoop up some meringue on top of tarts and repeat to fit as many mounds as possible on tarts.*
6. *Carefully brown meringue using a blowtorch or place under a hot broiler until golden brown.*
7. *Using the WIDE BLADE PEELER, shave chocolate curls over meringue if desired.*
8. *Serve tarts the same day they are made.*

FRUIT PIZZA

SLICES

Makes 1 pizza

Ingredients:

1 medium watermelon
1 kiwi
4 large strawberries
1/4 cup shredded coconut
1/4 cup blueberries

Method:

1. *Using the SANTOKU KNIFE, cut a 1-inch thick circle crosswise from the watermelon and save remainder of watermelon for another use.*

2. *Cut the watermelon circle into 8 even slices so that it looks like pizza then place on serving plate.*

3. *Using the WIDE BLADE PEELER, peel the kiwi then use the CRINKLE CHOPPER to cut into slices and place on the watermelon.*

4. *Using the LARGE CORER, create a tube shape from the strawberries then use the end of the TWIN CURL CUTTER to remove the strawberry tube from the LARGE CORER.*

5. *Using the SANTOKU KNIFE, slice strawberries in the shape of pepperoni then scatter over the watermelon.*

6. *Scatter the shredded coconut over the watermelon to look like cheese.*

7. *Top with blueberries and serve as desired.*

FALL RELISH TRAY

Makes 10-12 servings

Ingredients:

1 small pumpkin
1 English cucumber
3 very large carrots
1 bunch radishes
2 yellow squash
2 cups snap peas
2 cups small tomatoes
1 tub (16 ounces) garden vegetable dip

Method:

1. *Using the SANTOKU KNIFE, cut off the top from the pumpkin (figure 1).*
2. *Using the FRUIT AND VEGETABLE SCOOP, remove the strings and seeds from the pumpkin; set pumpkin aside.*
3. *Using the TWIN CURL CUTTER, twist out small spirals from the side of the cucumber (figure 2).*
4. *Using the WIDE BLADE PEELER, peel the carrots (figure 3) then use the CRINKLE CHOPPER to make carrot sticks.*
5. *Using the CRINKLE CHOPPER, cut the radishes and yellow squash into slices (figure 4).*
6. *Place the pumpkin in the center of a serving tray and fill with the vegetable dip.*
7. *Arrange prepared vegetables around the pumpkin on the tray, garnish as desired and serve.*

TIP

Make this relish tray really beautiful by using the WIDE BLADE PEELER to create pretty ribbons from a raw butternut squash and serve the ribbons along with the other veggies to dip.

ROUND MELON CUBE

Makes 1 serving

Ingredients:

1 small watermelon
1 cantaloupe
1 honeydew melon

Method:

1. *Using the SANTOKU KNIFE, cut each melon in half.*
2. *Using the FRUIT AND VEGETABLE SCOOP, remove the strings and seeds from the honeydew and cantaloupe.*
3. *Using the LARGE CORER, punch out cylinders from each melon then use the end of the TWIN CURL CUTTER to remove the melon cylinders from the LARGE CORER.*
4. *Using the SANTOKU KNIFE, slice thick, even coins from the cylinders.*
5. *Arrange the fruit into a stacked square on a plate.*
6. *Serve as desired.*

PRETZEL CHEESECAKE
SQUARES

Makes 8 servings

Ingredients:

1 honeydew melon
2 cups mini pretzels, crushed
4 tablespoons unsalted butter, melted
2 tablespoons granulated sugar
3 packages (8 ounces each) cream cheese, softened

1 cup powdered sugar
1 teaspoon vanilla extract
1 package (3 ounces) lime-flavored gelatin
1 cup boiling water
4 ice cubes

Method:

1. *Using the SANTOKU KNIFE, cut the honeydew melon in half.*
2. *Using the FRUIT AND VEGETABLE SCOOP, remove the seeds and strings from the melon.*
3. *Using the LEVER SCOOP, make melon balls and set aside.*
4. *In a bowl, stir together the pretzels, butter and sugar then pat into the bottom of an 8x8-inch dish.*
5. *In a mixing bowl, whisk together the cream cheese, powdered sugar and vanilla until smooth.*
6. *Spoon cream cheese mixture over the pretzel mixture then spread until smooth.*
7. *Add the melon balls, domed-side up, into the cream cheese mixture then refrigerate for 1 hour.*
8. *In a small bowl, stir together gelatin and boiling water until dissolved then stir in ice cubes until they melt; pour over cream cheese mixture and melon balls then refrigerate for an additional 2 hours.*
9. *Serve as desired.*

FRUIT CONES

Makes 4 servings

Ingredients:

1 cantaloupe
1 honeydew
1 watermelon
4 large flat-bottomed ice cream cones
4 mint sprigs

Method:

1. *Using the SANTOKU KNIFE, cut each melon in half.*
2. *Using the FRUIT AND VEGETABLE SCOOP, remove the strings and seeds from the cantaloupe and honeydew.*
3. *Using the LEVER SCOOP, make balls from each melon, saving remaining melons for another use.*
4. *Place the balls in the ice cream cones, pressing the balls onto the lip of the cones to secure.*
5. *Add mint sprigs and serve as desired.*

LADY BUG
CAPRESE

Makes 3 servings

Ingredients:
1 fresh mozzarella cheese ball
Kosher salt to taste
3 large basil leaves
3 Campari tomatoes
3 black olives
Store-bought balsamic glaze

Method:

1. *Using the SANTOKU KNIFE, cut slices from the mozzarella balls then place on serving plates.*
2. *Sprinkle salt over the mozzarella then place a basil leaf on top of each cheese piece.*
3. *Using the SANTOKU KNIFE, cut each tomato in half then cut a slit for the lady bug's "wings".*
4. *Place tomato halves on top of basil leaves.*
5. *Using the SANTOKU KNIFE, cut olives into halves then place by tomatoes to make the lady bug's "heads."*
6. *Using the pointed tip of the TWIN CURL CUTTER, place dots of balsamic glaze on tomatoes to make the lady bug's "spots".*
7. *Serve as desired with additional balsamic glaze.*

FRUIT CHRISTMAS TREE

Makes 10 servings

Ingredients:

1 medium watermelon
4 kiwi
1/2 of a cantaloupe
1 bunch kale
Assorted bunches of grapes
2 pint baskets strawberries
1 pint basket fresh figs
1 pint basket raspberries

Method:

1. *Using the SANTOKU KNIFE, cut the top and bottom off the watermelon then cut off all the rind.*

2. *Stand watermelon on one end then use the SANTOKU KNIFE to carve watermelon into a cone shape (figure 1) and place on serving tray. Reserve any remaining watermelon for another use.*

3. *Peel the kiwi using the WIDE BLADE PEELER then use the CRINKLE CHOPPER to cut the kiwi into 1/2-inch thick slices.*

4. *Using the FRUIT AND VEGETABLE SCOOP, remove the strings and seeds from the cantaloupe.*

5. *Using the LEVER SCOOP, make balls from the cantaloupe then use the SANTOKU KNIFE to carve a star from a piece of the rind (figure 2).*

6. *Tuck the kale under the bottom edge of the watermelon cone then place grapes around it.*

7. *Assemble the tree by attaching the fruits to the watermelon using wooden picks (figure 3).*

8. *Skewer the cantaloupe star on top of the tree (figure 4).*

9. *Serve as desired.*

TIP

If you don't want to buy so many different fruits, make this tree using only watermelon balls. The uniform color and shape of the balls creates a very elegant looking version of this tree and is a great way to use up watermelon trimmings.

CUCUMBER SMOKED SALMON CUPS

Makes 6-8 servings

Ingredients:

2 large and thick cucumbers
1 tub (8 ounces) smoked salmon-flavored cream cheese, softened
1 package smoked salmon
A few sprigs fresh dill

Method:

1. *Use the wavy edge of the VEGETABLE CURLER to decoratively score cucumbers lengthwise.*
2. *Using the CRINKLE CHOPPER, cut cucumbers crosswise into 1-inch pieces.*
3. *Using the LEVER SCOOP, remove the center of each cucumber piece to create a cup.*
4. *Place cucumber cups on a serving plate.*
5. *Place cream cheese into a zipper top bag, snip off one corner then pipe cream cheese into the cucumber cups.*
6. *Top each cup with a small piece of smoked salmon and a tiny sprig of dill.*
7. *Serve as desired.*

EASY RAMEN WITH
SOFT EGGS

Makes 2 servings

Ingredients:

2 large eggs
2 green onions
1 small carrot
A few asparagus spears
1 bell pepper
1 cup leftover roast chicken
2 packages chicken-flavored ramen noodles (with seasoning packets)

Method:

1. *Fill a saucepan halfway with water then bring to a boil over high heat.*
2. *While water is heating, place eggs in a bowl of warm water to temper them.*
3. *When water is boiling, gently add eggs and boil for exactly 6 minutes.*
4. *Remove eggs then place in ice water, stirring them around the water for a few minutes.*
5. *Gently crack large end of egg and peel carefully as egg centers are still soft; set aside.*
6. *Using the 8-BLADE SLICER, make long, pretty strands from the green onions.*
7. *Using the WIDE BLADE PEELER, peel the carrot then use the CRINKLE CHOPPER to cut thin slices from the carrot.*
8. *Using the SANTOKU KNIFE, slice the asparagus and bell pepper.*
9. *Place ramen noodles and seasoning packets into each of two bowls then top with the prepared ingredients, ending with the eggs and green onions on top.*
10. *Pour a cup of boiling water over the top of each bowl.*
11. *Let stand for 2-3 minutes to "cook" noodles and heat contents through.*
12. *Cut open the eggs and serve as desired.*

CHOCOLATE KIWI
LOLLIPOPSICLES

Makes 4 servings

Ingredients:

2 kiwi
Popsicle sticks
2 cups chocolate chips
2 tablespoons coconut oil

Method:

1. *Using the SANTOKU KNIFE, cut off the ends from the kiwi.*
2. *Using the WIDE BLADE PEELER, peel each kiwi.*
3. *Using the CRINKLE CHOPPER, cut 1-inch thick pieces from each kiwi.*
4. *Skewer each piece with a small popsicle stick and refrigerate for 15 minutes.*
5. *Combine chocolate chips and coconut oil in a microwave-safe bowl.*
6. *Microwave in 1 minute intervals, stirring well in between, until melted and smooth.*
7. *Dip each kiwi pop into the chocolate until completely covered then place on parchment paper.*
8. *Freeze pops for 1 hour before serving.*

EGGS IN
BELL PEPPER RINGS

Makes 4 servings

Ingredients:

2 bell peppers	Olive oil for the pan
1 Roma tomato	4 large eggs
1 green onion	Kosher salt and fresh pepper

Method:

1. *Using the LARGE CORER, remove stem, seeds and ribs from the bell peppers.*
2. *Using the SANTOKU KNIFE, slice the peppers into 1/2-inch thick rings.*
3. *Using the SANTOKU KNIFE, slice the tomato in half lengthwise.*
4. *Using the LEVER SCOOP, remove all seeds and watery part of the tomato then dice the tomato using the SANTOKU KNIFE.*
5. *Using the 8-BLADE SLICER, cut long strands from the green onion.*
6. *Preheat some oil in a skillet over medium heat.*
7. *Place as many pepper rings into the skillet as will fit then crack an egg into each ring.*
8. *Season with salt and pepper then sprinkle with tomatoes and green onions.*
9. *Cook until desired doneness then remove and repeat with any remaining rings.*
10. *Garnish as desired and serve.*

BACON POPPERS

Makes 6-8 servings

Ingredients:

24 large jalapeño peppers
1 cup Cheddar cheese, shredded
12 bacon slices
2 tablespoons honey

Method:

1. *Preheat oven to 450°F.*
2. *Wearing gloves, use the SMALL CORER to remove the core and seeds of each jalapeño pepper then hollow out or create an open channel with the SMALL CORER and remove the stem if desired.*
3. *Press cheese firmly into the peppers.*
4. *Using the SANTOKU KNIFE, cut bacon slices in half then wrap each pepper with bacon.*
5. *Place the peppers on a parchment-lined sheet pan.*
6. *Drizzle peppers with honey then bake for 20-25 minutes or until browned and bubbly.*
7. *Remove, garnish as desired and serve immediately.*

BUFFALO WINGS

Makes 4 servings

Ingredients:

2 celery stalks
24 chicken wings
Kosher salt and fresh pepper to taste
1 cup bottled wing sauce, divided
1/4 cup blue cheese, crumbled
Blue cheese and/or ranch dressing for serving

Method:

1. *Using the 8-BLADE SLICER, cut long, thin strands of celery. If the celery is very thick, use the SANTOKU KNIFE to cut celery in half horizontally before using the 8-BLADE SLICER.*

2. *Place celery strands in cold water for 30 minutes to allow them to curl.*

3. *Preheat oven to 450°F.*

4. *Using the SANTOKU KNIFE, cut apart chicken wings if they are whole then place on a foil-covered sheet pan.*

5. *Season with salt and pepper then drizzle with 1/2 cup wing sauce.*

6. *Cook for 25 minutes, turn wings over then cook for an additional 5-10 minutes or until well browned, crisp and temperature reaches 165°F on a meat thermometer.*

7. *Serve topped with remaining wing sauce, celery curls, blue cheese and/or Ranch dressing.*

LETTUCE TACOS WITH CORN SALSA

Makes 3-4 servings

Ingredients:
1 large head romaine lettuce
Sour cream for serving

For the Filling:
1 package (8 ounces) white mushrooms
1 bunch green onions
2 tomatoes
2 teaspoons olive oil
1 can (14 ounces) black beans, rinsed
1 tablespoon taco seasoning or to taste

For the Salsa:
2 ears fresh corn
1 small jalapeño pepper
A small handful of cilantro
Zest and juice of 1 lime
Kosher salt to taste

Method:

1. Using the SANTOKU KNIFE, trim the lettuce then save smaller leaves for another use; set aside.

2. Using the CRINKLE CHOPPER, chop up the mushrooms and green onions.

3. Using the SANTOKU KNIFE, dice the tomatoes.

4. Preheat the oil in a large skillet over medium-high heat.

5. Add the mushrooms and green onions to the skillet. Sauté for 3-4 minutes then add the beans, tomatoes as well as taco seasoning and cook for 2-3 minutes or until heated through and beans are hot; remove from heat.

6. Over a mixing bowl, use the CORN ZIPPER to remove the kernels.

7. Using the SMALL CORER, remove the stem and seeds from the jalapeño pepper then chop it using the SANTOKU KNIFE and add to the mixing bowl.

8. Using the SANTOKU SHEARS, roughly snip the cilantro then add to corn mixture along with the lime zest and juice.

9. Season with salt then serve tacos by using the lettuce as shells and filling them with mushroom mixture, salsa and a bit of sour cream.

MANGO
RIBBON TART

Makes 4 servings

Ingredients:

1 package (14.1 ounces) refrigerated pie crust
1 box (4 ounces) vanilla pudding mix
2 cups half & half
The seeds from 1 vanilla bean (optional)
3 ripe but firm mangoes
1/4 cup apple jelly

Method:

1. *Preheat oven to 350°F and apply nonstick cooking spray to a tart pan.*
2. *Unroll a pie crust (you may not need both crusts from the box) and press crust into tart pan (if your tart pan is rectangular you may need to patch pieces into corners).*
3. *Using the SANTOKU SHEARS, trim off any excess dough.*
4. *Bake for 20-25 minutes or until golden brown then remove and let cool.*
5. *Prepare pudding according to packaging instructions using half & half and vanilla bean instead of milk as stated in the pudding instructions; pour pudding into cooled crust.*
6. *Using the WIDE BLADE PEELER, peel pretty slices from the mangoes then coil up each slice.*
7. *Tuck coiled up mango slices into the pudding until tart is full.*
8. *Microwave the jelly for 30 seconds or until fluid then brush jelly over the top of the mango.*
9. *Garnish as desired and serve tart the same day it is made.*

CAPRESE STUFFED TOMATOES

Makes 4 servings

Ingredients:

8 small Campari tomatoes
Kosher salt to taste
A handful of basil leaves
1/2 cup fresh mini mozzarella balls
Extra-virgin olive oil for serving
Bottled balsamic glaze for serving
Fresh pepper to taste

Method:

1. Using the SANTOKU KNIFE, cut off the top from each tomato then cut off a tiny slice from the bottom so that the tomatoes sit flat and do not roll away.
2. Remove the center from each tomato using the LEVER SCOOP or SMALL CORER.
3. Season the center of each tomato with salt then arrange on a serving plate.
4. Using the 8-BLADE SLICER, julienne some of the basil leaves then tuck a whole basil leaf partially into each tomato.
5. Fill tomato centers with mozzarella balls (save any extra balls for other use).
6. Scatter the julienned basil over the tops then drizzle with oil and balsamic glaze.
7. Season with salt and pepper and serve as desired.

RAINBOW RELISH TRAY

Makes 8-10 servings

For the Ranch Dip:

1/2 cup packed basil, parsley and dill leaves
2 garlic cloves
1 bunch green onions
1 tub (8 ounces) sour cream
1/2 cup mayonnaise
Kosher salt and fresh pepper to taste
1 tablespoon white vinegar
1/2 cup Parmesan cheese, grated

For the Veggies:

1/2 head red cabbage
3 cucumbers
3 yellow bell peppers
4 carrots
2 packages small tomatoes

Method:

1. *Combine the herbs, garlic and green onions then chop finely using the SANTOKU KNIFE.*
2. *Scrape into a mixing bowl then add remaining dip ingredients; stir well and chill.*
3. *Using the CRINKLE CHOPPER, cut decorative shreds from the cabbage; set aside.*
4. *Using the TWIN CURL CUTTER, twist out spirals from the side of the cucumbers.*
5. *Using the LARGE CORER, remove the stem, seeds and pith from the bell peppers.*
6. *Using the CRINKLE CHOPPER, cut the bell peppers into strips.*
7. *Using the WIDE BLADE PEELER, peel the carrots then use the CRINKLE CHOPPER to cut them into strips.*
8. *To assemble, pour the dip in a serving bowl at the bottom of your serving plate.*
9. *Arrange the cabbage, cucumber, bell peppers, carrots as well as tomatoes in a semi-circle around the bowl and serve.*

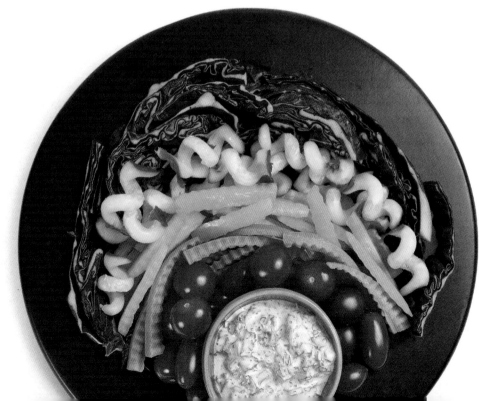

39

INSIDE OUT
CARAMEL APPLES

Makes 2-4 servings

Ingredients:

2 envelopes (1/4 ounce each) unflavored gelatin
1/4 cup apple juice
1 cup bottled caramel sauce
2 large apples

Method:

1. *Whisk the gelatin into the apple juice in a microwave-safe bowl then set aside for 5 minutes.*
2. *Microwave the apple juice mixture for 1 minute or until hot and all gelatin is dissolved.*
3. *Stir in the caramel sauce and set aside to cool until just warm.*
4. *Using the SANTOKU KNIFE, cut each apple in half (figure 1) then cut off a slice from the curved part so that the apple halves stand level.*
5. *Using the LEVER SCOOP, remove the apple cores (figure 2).*
6. *Using the LEVER SCOOP, remove most of the apple flesh, leaving a 1/4-inch thick wall (figure 3).*
7. *Place apple halves on a small sheet pan then place in the fridge.*
8. *Carefully pour gelatin mixture into each apple half until full then chill for 2 hours (figure 4).*
9. *When ready to serve, use the CRINKLE CHOPPER to trim off browned apple edges if desired or necessary then cut each apple into wedges and serve as desired.*

RECIPES

TIP

Add a layer of chopped, toasted pecans or walnuts to the top of the caramel-gelatin mixture before it sets to create a different look and delicious crunch.

BEST CREAMED CORN

Makes 4-6 servings

Ingredients:

6 ears fresh sweet corn
3 tablespoons unsalted butter
1 tablespoon granulated sugar
Kosher salt and fresh pepper to taste
6 bacon strips, cooked

Method:

1. *Holding each ear over a large skillet, remove all corn kernels using the CORN ZIPPER.*
2. *Using the FRUIT AND VEGETABLE SCOOP, scrape the cobs of all remaining corn bits and juice.*
3. *Add remaining ingredients, except bacon, to the skillet then set over medium-high heat.*
4. *Stir constantly until bubbly and starch in the corn has thickened the creamed corn.*
5. *Using the CRINKLE CHOPPER, dice up the bacon strips, place on corn, garnish as desired and serve.*

LOADED BAKED

SWEET POTATO

Makes 3 servings

Ingredients:

3 sweet potatoes
1 small yellow onion
8 ounces white mushrooms
8 ounces kale

Kosher salt and fresh pepper to taste
2 tablespoons olive oil
1/3 cup ricotta cheese

Method:

1. *Preheat oven to 375°F.*
2. *Place the potatoes on a sheet pan then poke a hole in each one using the pointed end of the TWIN CURL CUTTER.*
3. *Bake the potatoes in the oven for 1 hour or until soft.*
4. *Using the CRINKLE CHOPPER, slice the onion, mushrooms and kale then place them in a bowl.*
5. *Add the salt, pepper and oil to the onion mixture and toss to coat evenly.*
6. *Make a foil pouch, put the onion mixture in it then add pouch to the oven during the last 30 minutes of the potatoes baking.*
7. *When potatoes are done baking, remove potatoes and vegetable pouch from the oven.*
8. *Using the SANTOKU KNIFE, slit potatoes open then top with the pouch contents.*
9. *Top with a dollop of ricotta, garnish as desired and serve.*

CALIFORNIA ROLL
SUSHI CONES

Makes 4 servings

Ingredients:

1 bag (12 ounces) short grain white rice
1 teaspoon kosher salt
1 teaspoon granulated sugar
2 teaspoons rice vinegar
1 package (4 ounces) surimi imitation crab
1 avocado
1 small carrot
1 cucumber
Nori seaweed sheets
1 teaspoon sesame seeds, toasted
Soy sauce, pickled ginger and wasabi for serving

Method:

1. *Wash rice in a strainer several times using cold water then drain and transfer to a rice cooker.*
2. *Add 12 ounces water to rice cooker (same ratio of rice and water if you are cooking a different amount of rice) then cook until done.*
3. *Spread cooked rice out on a plastic wrap lined sheet pan.*
4. *Sprinkle rice as evenly as possible with salt, sugar and vinegar then toss to cool.*
5. *Set rice aside then use the SANTOKU KNIFE to slice the crab into small bites.*
6. *Using the SANTOKU KNIFE, cut the avocado in half.*
7. *Using the FRUIT AND VEGETABLE SCOOP remove the pit and the flesh from the avocado.*
8. *Using the SANTOKU KNIFE, thinly slice the removed avocado flesh.*
9. *Using the WIDE BLADE PEELER, peel the carrot then use the VEGETABLE CURLER to make carrot curls.*
10. *Using the TWIN CURL CUTTER, twist out spirals from the cucumber.*
11. *Shape cones with the nori and fill each with some of the rice, crab, avocado, carrot and cucumber.*
12. *Sprinkle with sesame seeds then serve with soy sauce, pickled ginger, wasabi and remaining carrot curls.*

TIP

The use of a rice cooker is highly recommended because the rice grains turn out drier and fluffier than cooking rice on the stovetop.

LEMON RICOTTA COOKIES

Makes 24 cookies

Ingredients:

1/2 cup unsalted butter, softened
2 cups granulated sugar
2 large eggs
1 tub (15 ounces) whole milk ricotta cheese
Zest and juice from 1 lemon
2 1/2 cups all purpose flour
1 teaspoon baking powder
1/2 teaspoon kosher salt
Powdered sugar for dusting

Method:

1. *Preheat oven to 375°F.*
2. *In a large mixing bowl, combine the butter and sugar using a hand mixer until well blended.*
3. *Add the eggs, ricotta, lemon zest and juice then mix until uniform in color.*
4. *Using low speed, mix in the flour, baking powder and salt just until incorporated.*
5. *Using the LEVER SCOOP, portion the dough onto parchment-lined sheet pans.*
6. *Bake the cookies for 12-15 minutes or until edges just start to turn golden.*
7. *Remove and let cool.*
8. *Sift a heavy layer of powdered sugar over cookies, garnish as desired and serve.*

CORN FRITTERS

Makes 6-8 servings

Ingredients:

2 ears fresh corn
2 tablespoons unsalted butter, melted
1 teaspoon vanilla extract
1/2 cup buttermilk
1/4 cup granulated sugar
1 1/2 cups all purpose flour

1 1/2 teaspoons kosher salt
2 teaspoons baking powder
2 large eggs
3 cups canola oil for frying
Powdered sugar for serving

Method:

1. *Using the CORN ZIPPER, remove all corn kernels from the cobs into a large mixing bowl.*
2. *Add remaining ingredients, except oil and powdered sugar, and mix until blended.*
3. *Preheat the oil in a large heavy-bottomed pot over medium heat.*
4. *Using a thermometer, monitor the oil temperature until it reaches 350°F.*
5. *Using the LEVER SCOOP, drop batter carefully into the hot oil.*
6. *Fry 4-5 fritters at a time for 2-4 minutes, turning them over halfway through frying, until golden brown.*
7. *Remove and let drain on a wire rack set over absorbent paper on a sheet pan.*
8. *Repeat with remaining batter.*
9. *Top with powdered sugar and serve hot.*

TIP

Use an electric deep fryer to make these quickly and efficiently.

APPLE CANDLE DECORATION

Makes 3 decorations

Ingredients:

3 apples or as many as desired (any color)
3 votive candles or as many as desired

Method:

1. *Insert the LARGE CORER 1-inch deep into the top of each apple.*
2. *Using the LEVER SCOOP, remove the cut apple circle.*
3. *Using the SANTOKU BLADE, trim the bottom of each apple so they sit flat.*
4. *Insert a votive candle into the top of each apple.*
5. *Place on a non-flammable surface that is safe to use with candles and candle wax.*
6. *Use as desired.*

APPETIZER
ALLIGATOR

Makes 4-6 servings

Ingredients:

1 large English cucumber
1 Roma tomato
8 ounces mini mozzarella balls
2 whole cloves
Small bamboo skewers or wooden picks
1 Swiss cheese block (8 ounces)
1 pint small tomatoes
2 large carrots

Method:

1. *Using the SANTOKU BLADE, cut off a lengthwise slice from the cucumber so that the cucumber can stay in place.*

2. *Using the SANTOKU BLADE cut four alligator feet from the sliced off cucumber piece then cut a slit for the mouth into one end of the cucumber and carve the teeth.*

3. *Using the SANTOKU BLADE, cut a thin slice from the Roma tomato to make the "tongue".*

4. *Using the SMALL CORER, trim the mozzarella balls into "eyeballs" then insert the whole cloves as "pupils" before attaching assembled "eyes" to the cucumber with skewers.*

5. *Using the CRINKLE CHOPPER, cut the Swiss cheese into cubes.*

6. *Assemble mini kebabs with the cheese cubes and tomatoes using skewers.*

7. *Insert skewers along the alligator's back.*

8. *Using the WIDE BLADE PEELER, peel the carrots then use the VEGETABLE CURLER to make curls.*

9. *Place the carrot curls around the alligator.*

10. *Serve as desired.*

KIWI
TURTLES

Makes 2 servings

Ingredients:
1 kiwi
5 green grapes

Method:
1. *Using the SANTOKU KNIFE, cut off each end from the kiwi.*
2. *Using the WIDE BLADE PEELER, peel kiwi then use the CRINKLE CHOPPER to cut them into 1-inch thick slices.*
3. *Using the SANTOKU KNIFE, cut 2 of the grapes into quarters for the "legs".*
4. *Cut one of the grapes into slivers to make the turtle "tails".*
5. *Use the pointed end of the TWIN CURL CUTTER to pry out 4 kiwi seeds from the scraps for the turtle's "eyes".*
6. *Wipe any remaining kiwi off of the seeds to be used as "eyes" then stick them to the top of two of the grapes.*
7. *Place kiwi on small serving plates then assemble into turtles by pressing on heads, legs and tails as pictured.*

APPLES WITH GUMMY WORMS

Makes 2 servings

Ingredients:

2 apples
2 tablespoons marshmallow fluff
2 gummy worms
2 green gumdrops
2 graham crackers, crumbled

Method:

1. *Using the SMALL CORER, cut a hole in the side of each apple.*
2. *Using the SANTOKU KNIFE, cut the apple in half horizontally, making sure to cut through the hole.*
3. *Using the LEVER SCOOP, create a divot in each apple half then fill with marshmallow fluff.*
4. *Place tops back on apples then insert a gummy worm into each small hole.*
5. *Pinch each gumdrop until flat then use the SANTOKU KNIFE to cut into a leaf shape.*
6. *Insert gumdrop leaves next to stems in apple tops.*
7. *Place graham crumbs on a serving plate or tray then place apple on top and serve.*

BOO HALLOWEEN
PUMPKIN

Makes 1 pumpkin

Ingredients:
1 pumpkin or other squash
1 battery-powered light or glow stick

Method:
1. *Using the pointed end of the TWIN CURL CUTTER like a pencil, score top of pumpkin and side where you would like the word "BOO" to be.*
2. *Using the SANTOKU KNIFE, cut off and reserve the top.*
3. *Using the FRUIT AND VEGETABLE SCOOP, hollow out the pumpkin, removing the stings and seeds.*
4. *Using the SMALL/LARGE CORERS, punch out the word "BOO" on the side of the pumpkin.*
5. *Insert the battery-powered light or glow stick then replace top and use as desired.*

BENTO BOX KID LUNCH

Makes 1 serving

Ingredients:

1 small apple
3 strawberries
1 small carrot
1 small cucumber
1 hotdog
A few dry spaghetti noodles
Ketchup for serving

Method:

1. *Using the TWIN CURL CUTTER, twist out spirals from the apple.*
2. *Using the 8-BLADE SLICER, cut the strawberry into fans.*
3. *Using the WIDE BLADE PEELER, peel the carrot then make curls using the VEGETABLE CURLER.*
4. *Using the VEGETABLE CURLER, make curls from the cucumber.*
5. *Pour some water in a microwave safe 4-cup container and bring to a boil in the microwave.*
6. *Using the SANTOKU KNIFE, cut the hotdogs into bite-size pieces.*
7. *Break spaghetti into 4-inch lengths then insert 8 pieces of spaghetti through each hotdog piece.*
8. *Place the hotdog/pasta pieces in the boiling water and place in microwave for 8-10 minutes or until pasta is tender.*
9. *Remove from microwave then run cool water over it for a few seconds.*
10. *Place all in a Bento box or divided plate and serve with ketchup for dipping.*

53

CHEESE WEDDING CAKE

Makes 1 cake

Ingredients:
3 wheels of Brie cheese in 10-inch, 6-inch and 3-inch diameters
2 carrots
2 parsnips
2 zucchini
2 leeks
1 bunch fresh sage
1 bunch fresh rosemary

Method:
1. *Stack the cheeses on a serving tray or pedestal.*
2. *Using the WIDE BLADE PEELER, peel the carrots and parsnips.*
3. *Using the VEGETABLE CURLER, make different size curls from the carrots, parsnips and zucchini.*
4. *For some of the flowers, drag the crinkle part of the VEGETABLE CURLER down the vegetables first to create a spider mum type flower.*
5. *Using the SANTOKU KNIFE, cut leeks into 2-inch lengths.*
6. *Using the 8-BLADE SLICER, make cuts all around leek pieces then put in cold water to allot for cuts to curl open.*
7. *Secure flowers, leeks and herbs together using wooden picks then place on the "cake".*
8. *Cover with damp paper towels and refrigerate until ready to serve.*

TIP
You can use different types of cheeses sold in a "wheel" shape to make different looking cakes.

APPLE & PEANUT BUTTER SPIRALS

Makes 1-2 servings

Ingredients:

2 firm apples
3 tablespoons smooth peanut butter
1 tablespoon honey

Method:

1. *Using the TWIN CURL CUTTER, twist out spirals from each apple.*
2. *Save remaining apple scraps for another use or discard.*
3. *In a small bowl, stir together the peanut butter and honey to make a dip or serve spirals with both separately.*

TIP

Honey Crisp apples are a good choice to make ahead the spirals as they tend to not turn brown as quickly as other types of apples.

RAW BUTTERNUT
RIBBON SALAD

Makes 4 servings

Ingredients:

1 tablespoon Dijon mustard
Kosher salt and fresh pepper to taste
3 tablespoons red wine vinegar
2 tablespoons honey
2 tablespoons olive oil

1 butternut squash
2 green onions
1/2 cup raisins or craisins
1/4 cup feta or blue cheese, crumbled
1/4 cup pecans, toasted

Method:

1. *In a large mixing bowl, whisk together the mustard, salt, pepper, vinegar and honey.*
2. *While whisking, stream in the oil until combined then set aside.*
3. *Using the SANTOKU KNIFE, cut off the ends from the squash.*
4. *Using the WIDE BLADE PEELER, peel the squash then peel into pretty ribbons, turning it as you go until you have peeled all but the seedy center; discard center.*
5. *Place ribbons into the mixing bowl with the mustard mixture.*
6. *Using the 8-BLADE SLICER, make long, thin strips of green onions then add to the bowl.*
7. *Add remaining ingredients to the bowl then toss to coat with the dressing.*
8. *Let stand for 15 minutes to soften the squash, transfer to serving plate, garnish as desired and serve.*

MINI CARAMEL APPLES

Makes 4 servings

Ingredients:

4 apples
Small wooden picks or lollipop sticks
1/2 cup pecans, toasted
1 cup jarred caramel sauce
Sprinkles or jimmies as desired

Method:

1. *Using the LEVER SCOOP, remove as many balls as possible from each apple.*
2. *Skewer each ball through the skin side then place on a serving tray.*
3. *Using the SANTOKU KNIFE, finely chop pecans then transfer to a small bowl.*
4. *Pour caramel sauce into a separate small bowl.*
5. *Pour sprinkles into a third small bowl.*
6. *Arrange all items on the serving platter.*
7. *Dip each apple ball first in caramel then dip in nuts and/or sprinkles before serving.*

SALSA SALAD CUBES

Makes 6-8 servings

Ingredients:
2 English cucumbers
2 carrots
1 cup fresh salsa
1 green onion

Method:

1. *Using the SANTOKU KNIFE, cut cucumbers into 1 1/2-inch cubes and trim off peel if desired.*
2. *Using the SMALL CORER, make a hole into one side of each cube then place on a serving tray.*
3. *Using the WIDE BLADE PEELER, peel the carrots then twist through the VEGETABLE CURLER to make carrot ruffles.*
4. *Coil up the carrot ruffles then insert one into each cucumber cube hole.*
5. *Fill centers of carrot curls with salsa.*
6. *Using the 8-BLADE SLICER, slice the green onions then sprinkle over cubes.*
7. *Garnish as desired and serve.*

TIP
This elegant appetizer is perfect to serve when watching calories and trying to consume more vegetables.

WATERMELON
KETTLE GRILL

Makes 1 kettle grill

Ingredients:

1 small watermelon
1 small zucchini
3 thick celery stalks
2 baskets fresh blackberries
1 small honeydew melon
1 small cantaloupe
Skewers

Method:

1. *Using the SANTOKU KNIFE, horizontally cut the top third off of the watermelon.*
2. *Using the FRUIT AND VEGETABLE SCOOP, remove all of the flesh from the watermelon.*
3. *Using the SANTOKU KNIFE, cut a small end from the zucchini and attach it to the top of the smaller watermelon piece using a wooden pick (figure 1).*
4. *Thread 5-6 bamboo skewers about 1/2-inch below the opening of the large watermelon piece and in 1-inch intervals to look like grill grates (figure 2).*
5. *Using the SANTOKU SHEARS, trim the skewer ends if needed.*
6. *Using the SANTOKU KNIFE, trim the celery stalks and run a bamboo skewer through them lengthwise. Attach to the bottom of the grill base, trimming skewers as needed (figure 3).*
7. *Remove center skewer (grill grate), pour the blackberries into the watermelon to look like charcoal briquettes then replace center skewer.*
8. *Using the SANTOKU KNIFE, cut the cantaloupe in half then use the FRUIT AND VEGETABLE SCOOP to remove the strings and seeds; repeat with honeydew melon.*
9. *Using the LEVER SCOOP, make balls from the watermelon, cantaloupe and honeydew.*
10. *Make fruit kebabs using bamboo skewers and balls then place on the grill grates.*
11. *Use a bamboo skewer to attach the small watermelon piece to the grill to look like an open lid (figure 4).*
12. *Serve as desired.*

CARROT RIBBON CHIPS

Makes 4 servings

Ingredients:

8 large carrots
2 tablespoons olive oil
Kosher salt and fresh pepper to taste
A few sprigs fresh thyme leaves

Method:

1. *Preheat oven to 300°F.*
2. *Using the WIDE BLADE PEELER, peel the carrots then peel long, pretty ribbons from all carrots.*
3. *In a large mixing bowl, toss together carrots and remaining ingredients.*
4. *Divide ribbons between two parchment-lined sheet pans, separating ribbons so that they don't touch.*
5. *Bake for 30-40 minutes or until crispy and lightly browned.*
6. *Turn oven off, keep sheet pans of carrots inside oven and leave door ajar for 30 minutes to allow ribbons to continue to dry out and become crispy.*
7. *Remove, serve as desired and store leftovers in an airtight container at room temperature for up to 2 days.*

RECIPES

APPLE PIE
FRIES

Makes 6-8 servings

Ingredients:

1 box (14.1 ounces) refrigerated pie dough
2 tablespoons granulated sugar
1/2 teaspoon ground cinnamon
1/2 cup store-bought caramel sauce for serving

Method:

1. *Preheat oven to 350°F.*
2. *Using the SANTOKU SHEARS, cut open the bag of pie dough from the box.*
3. *Unroll 1 pie dough circle onto a parchment-lined sheet pan.*
4. *Dampen the top of the dough using a pastry brush and water.*
5. *Sprinkle dough surface with the sugar and cinnamon.*
6. *Using the CRINKLE CHOPPER, cut French fry size sticks from the pie dough.*
7. *Slightly pull apart each dough stick so they don't stick together.*
8. *Bake for 10-15 minutes or until golden brown then remove and let cool.*
9. *Serve warm or cold with caramel sauce.*

FROG SANDWICH

Makes 1 serving

Ingredients:

4 whole wheat sandwich bread slices
2 Swiss cheese slices
3 deli ham slices
2 teaspoons mayonnaise

1 green grape
1 dark raisin
1 cucumber

Method:

1. *To assemble sandwiches, spread mayonnaise on 2 bread slices, top each with a slice of cheese and a slice of ham then place other bread slices on top.*

2. *Cut the sandwiches with a drinking glass or cookie cutter into circles then stack sandwiches on top of each other.*

3. *Using the SANTOKU KNIFE, cut the grape diagonally in half then place on top of sandwich stack to make the frog's "eyes".*

4. *Cut the raisin in half then attach the sticky cut side to the top of each grape half to complete the "eyeballs".*

5. *Using the SANTOKU KNIFE, cut a thin slice of cucumber into 8 wedges then place around sandwich on a serving plate to make the frog's "toes".*

6. *Using the SANTOKU KNIFE, cut a thin slice from the remaining ham to make the frog's "tongue" then roll up the ham slice halfway and attach to the sandwich stack as the "tongue".*

7. *Using the TWIN CURL CUTTER, twist out spirals from remaining cucumber.*

8. *Serve frog with cucumber curls on the side.*

AVOCADO TURKEY
MELTS

Makes 4 servings

Ingredients:

1 avocado

4 whole grain bread slices, toasted

4 pepperoncini peppers

12 ounces roast turkey slices

Kosher salt and fresh pepper to taste

2 tomatoes

2 handfuls of fresh spinach

4 Swiss or Provolone cheese slices

Method:

1. *Preheat broiler on high.*

2. *Using the SANTOKU KNIFE, slice the avocado in half.*

3. *Using the FRUIT AND VEGETABLE SCOOP, remove the avocado pit and the flesh from the skin.*

4. *Using the CRINKLE CHOPPER, slice the avocado thinly then divide between toast on a sheet pan.*

5. *Using the SANTOKU KNIFE, thinly slice the pepperoncini peppers and scatter over the avocado.*

6. *Roll up turkey slices then place on top and season to taste.*

7. *Using the SMALL CORER, remove the core from the tomatoes.*

8. *Using the SANTOKU KNIFE, thinly slice the tomato then place on top of turkey.*

9. *Place spinach and cheese over the tomatoes then place under the broiler for 2-3 minutes or until cheese is melted and begins to bubble.*

10. *Remove from broiler and serve hot.*

APPLE GRAPE CARS

Makes 16 cars

Ingredients:
1 red apple
1 green apple
Red grapes
Green grapes
Small skewers or wooden picks

Method:
1. *Using the CRINKLE CHOPPER, cut 8 wedges from each apple.*
2. *Using the LARGE CORER, remove the core from each slice.*
3. *Place a grape on one side of a skewer then push skewer through apple slice and attach another grape on the other side to make the "wheels".*
4. *Using the SANTOKU SHEARS, trim the ends of the skewers.*
5. *Repeat until all the apple cars have wheels.*
6. *Serve as desired.*

NOTE
Use caution when serving foods that contain wooden picks to children.

CHEESE & CORN
QUINOA BITES

Makes 4-6 servings

Ingredients:

2 cobs fresh corn
1 bunch green onions
2 cups quinoa, cooked
1 large egg
1 cup Parmesan cheese, grated
1 tablespoon bottled hot sauce or to taste
Kosher salt and fresh pepper to taste
Olive oil for sautéing

Method:

1. *Using the CORN ZIPPER, remove all corn kernels into a large mixing bowl.*
2. *Using the SANTOKU KNIFE, chop green onions, reserving a few of the green tops for garnish.*
3. *Using the 8-BLADE SLICER, cut long, pretty strands of the reserved green onion tops; set aside.*
4. *Add remaining ingredients, except oil and reserved green onion strands, to the bowl and stir thoroughly.*
5. *Preheat the oil in a large skillet over medium heat.*
6. *Using the LEVER SCOOP, drop portions of the corn mixture into the skillet and pat down tops to form small patties.*
7. *Sauté for 3-4 minutes on each side or until golden brown and crispy.*
8. *Remove and repeat with remaining mixture then top with green onion strands and serve.*

FLOWER ARRANGEMENT

Makes 1 arrangement

Ingredients:

1 butternut squash	2 parsnips
2 leeks	1 cucumber
Food coloring (if desired)	1 bunch radishes
2 bunches green onions	1 bunch fresh sage
2 carrots	1 bunch fresh rosemary

Method:

1. *Using the SANTOKU KNIFE, trim the bottom off the squash and cut off the top.*
2. *Using the LEVER SCOOP, hollow out the neck to create a "vase" (figure 1).*
3. *Using the SMALL CORER, make a polka dot pattern around the top of the squash.*
4. *Using the SANTOKU KNIFE, slice the leeks into 2-inch pieces, saving the green part to make the leaves.*
5. *Using the 8-BLADE SLICER, cut down the leek pieces to make petals without cutting all the way down or they will fall apart (figure 2).*
6. *Place leeks in cold water to allow them to open up (add food coloring to the water if desired).*
7. *Using the SANTOKU KNIFE, cut the reserved green part of the leeks and the green onions into flower stems and leaves; set aside.*
8. *Using the WIDE BLADE PEELER, peel the carrots, parsnips and cucumber, twist through the VEGETABLE CURLER (figure 3) then roll up into flowers.*
9. *Secure flowers using wooden picks.*
10. *Using the LEVER SCOOP, make round flower centers from butternut squash scraps then add to flowers.*
11. *Using the 8-BLADE SLICER, create a cross hatch pattern on the radishes then soak in cold water to allow them to open.*
12. *To assemble, use various length bamboo skewers threaded through green onions then add flowers to the end of the skewers (figure 4). Arrange in squash as desired, filling in with the reserved leek leaves, sage and rosemary.*
13. *Use water in a spray bottle to mist arrangement and wrap until needed.*

RECIPES

CUCUMBER ROLL UPS

Makes 6 servings

Ingredients:

2 English cucumbers
2 carrots
1 tub (8 ounces) garden vegetable flavored cream cheese, softened
Handful of fresh basil leaves

Method:

1. *Using the WIDE BLADE PEELER, make long ribbons from the cucumbers.*
2. *Using the WIDE BLADE PEELER, peel carrots then make long ribbons from the carrots.*
3. *Spread a thin layer of cream cheese on the cucumber ribbons.*
4. *Top each with 2 overlapping carrot ribbons, trying to make the carrot ribbons the same lengths as the cucumber ribbons then roll up into tight spirals, tucking a basil leaf halfway in as you roll; secure with picks.*
5. *Place on a serving plate with basil leaves sticking up and serve.*

EGG STUFFED
PEPPERS

Makes 4 servings

Ingredients:

4 large bell peppers
1 bag (9.6 ounces) hearty sausage crumbles, cooked
1 cup Cheddar cheese, shredded
1/2 cup ketchup or pasta sauce
4 large eggs
Kosher salt and fresh pepper to taste
1 green onion

Method:

1. *Preheat oven to 450°F.*
2. *Using the LARGE CORER, remove the core from the peppers.*
3. *Place peppers on a parchment-lined sheet pan.*
4. *In a mixing bowl, combine the sausage, cheese and ketchup or pasta sauce.*
5. *Spoon mixture into the peppers, leaving a 1/4-inch deep space for the egg.*
6. *Bake peppers for 25 minutes or until they begin to brown and bubble.*
7. *Remove from oven and crack an egg into each pepper top then season with salt and pepper.*
8. *Return to oven and bake for 5-10 minutes or until eggs are cooked to desired doneness.*
9. *Using the 8-BLADE SLICER, cut long, thin strands from the green onion then place over peppers.*
10. *Garnish as desired and serve.*

FOURTH OF JULY
BOAT

Makes 10 servings

Ingredients:

1 medium watermelon
1 golden Dewlicious melon or honeydew melon
1 cup sugar
Blue food coloring
2 cups white chocolate chips
2 pint baskets strawberries
2 pint baskets blueberries

Method:

1. *Using the SANTOKU KNIFE, trim the bottom off the watermelon so it sits flat (figure 1).*
2. *Using the end of the TWIN CURL CUTTER like a "pencil", sketch the 3 stars and 3 stripes into the side of the watermelon (figure 2).*
3. *Using the SANTOKU KNIFE, trim away the green flesh from the stars and stripes (figure 3).*
4. *Using the SANTOKU KNIFE, cut horizontally around the top part of the melon, avoiding the stars and stripes, then remove the top (figure 4).*
5. *Using the FRUIT AND VEGETABLE SCOOP, remove large pieces of the melon flesh.*
6. *Using the LEVER SCOOP, make balls from the watermelon and golden Dewlicious melon.*
7. *Place sugar in a plastic zipper top bag, add 3 drops blue food coloring and shake bag vigorously. Press the darker blue areas to help break them up and shake again until uniform in color; set aside.*
8. *Place white chocolate in a microwave-safe bowl, microwave for 1 minute, stir then microwave for an additional 1 minute and stir until melted.*
9. *Dip each strawberry 2/3 of the way into the melted chocolate.*
10. *Dip the chocolate-dipped strawberries 1/3 of the way into the blue sugar to make red, white and blue strawberries.*
11. *Stand skewers upright in a scrap piece of watermelon rind to dry.*
12. *Place melon boat on serving tray then arrange all fruits attractively in melon.*
13. *Press skewered strawberries into melon and serve as desired.*

FRUIT
POPSICLES

Makes 6 pops

Ingredients:

3 kiwi
1 cantaloupe
1/2 of a watermelon

1 pineapple
2 cups coconut water
2 tablespoons granulated sugar or other sweetener

Method:

1. *Place 6 small paper drinking cups or popsicle molds on a small sheet pan.*
2. *Using the WIDE BLADE PEELER, peel the kiwi.*
3. *Using the LEVER SCOOP, make 6 kiwi balls then place one in each cup.*
4. *Using the SANTOKU KNIFE, cut cantaloupe in half then use the FRUIT AND VEGETABLE SCOOP to remove seeds and strings.*
5. *Using the LARGE CORER, punch out tubes from the cantaloupe then use the end of the TWIN CURL CUTTER to remove the cantaloupe tubes from the LARGE CORER.*
6. *Using the SANTOKU KNIFE, slice the cantaloupe tubes into coins then add to cups.*
7. *Repeat cantaloupe method with the watermelon.*
8. *Using the SANTOKU KNIFE, remove the top, bottom and rind from the pineapple.*
9. *Using the CRINKLE CHOPPER, cut squares from the pineapple then place in cups.*
10. *Push a popsicle stick into the fruit in each cup.*
11. *Stir the coconut water and sugar together then pour into cups until almost full.*
12. *Freeze until solid then serve as desired.*

RECIPES

GOAT CHEESE POPPERS
WITH HONEY

Makes 6-8 servings

Ingredients:

12 ounces goat cheese
Kosher salt and fresh pepper to taste
1 green onion
1/2 cup walnuts, toasted
Handful of fresh parsley
Honey for serving

Method:

1. *In a mixing bowl, combine the goat cheese, salt and pepper.*
2. *Using the SANTOKU KNIFE, finely chop the green onion and walnuts then add to the bowl.*
3. *Stir cheese mixture well then use the LEVER SCOOP to make balls from the mixture.*
4. *Using the SANTOKU SHEARS, snip the parsley into small bits.*
5. *Roll each goat cheese ball lightly in the parsley then place on a serving tray.*
6. *Drizzle with honey when ready to serve.*

GRANOLA APPLE SAMMIES

Makes 1 serving

Ingredients:

1 apple
2 tablespoons peanut butter
2 tablespoons store-bought granola
2 teaspoons honey

Method:

1. *Using the CRINKLE CHOPPER, slice the apples into rounds.*
2. *Using the SMALL CORER, remove the cores from the apple rounds.*
3. *Spread peanut butter on half the apple rounds then top with granola and drizzle with honey.*
4. *Top each with another apple round to assemble the sammies.*
5. *Serve as desired.*

GREEN PEA HUMMUS
WITH DIPPERS

Makes 6-8 servings

For the Hummus:
1 avocado
2 cups frozen peas, thawed
1/4 cup mint leaves
2 green onions
1 tablespoon granulated sugar
Zest and juice from 1 lemon
1/2 cup canola oil
Kosher salt and fresh pepper to taste

Dippers:
2 large carrots
2 yellow squash
2 zucchini
12 Campari tomatoes

Method:

1. *Using the SANTOKU KNIFE, cut avocado in half.*
2. *Using the FRUIT AND VEGETABLE SCOOP, remove the pit and flesh from the avocado halves then place flesh into a food processor or blender; discard pit.*
3. *Add remaining hummus ingredients to blender and process until smooth.*
4. *Transfer hummus to a serving bowl.*
5. *Using the WIDE BLADE PEELER, peel the carrots then use the CRINKLE CHOPPER to cut them into coins.*
6. *Using the CRINKLE CHOPPER, cut the yellow squash in half lengthwise then cut into half moons.*
7. *Using the CRINKLE CHOPPER, cut zucchini into French fry shaped pieces.*
8. *Using the SMALL CORER, core the tomatoes if desired or leave whole.*
9. *Arrange the vegetables around the hummus and serve as desired.*

PINEAPPLE MARGARITA
PARROT

Makes 1 serving

Ingredients:

1 pineapple
1 carrot
Wooden skewers
2 whole cloves
2 cups ice cubes
2 cups margarita mix (with or without alcohol)

Method:

1. *Using the SANTOKU KNIFE, trim off the bottom from the pineapple so that it sits flat then cut off 3-inches from the top (figure 1).*

2. *Using the SANTOKU KNIFE, trim the pineapple rind then carve into a rough square to make the parrot's "head". Continue carving away to round the parrot's "face" (figure 2).*

3. *Using the SANTOKU SHEARS, trim green fronds into "tail feathers".*

4. *Using the WIDE BLADE PEELER, whittle a 2-inch piece of carrot into a "beak" then attach using wooden skewers (figure 3).*

5. *Using the FRUIT AND VEGETABLE SCOOP, hollow out the pineapple flesh from the pineapple around the core (figure 4).*

6. *Using the SANTOKU SHEARS, snip out the pineapple core.*

7. *Push 2 wooden skewers into the area along the pineapple fronds where the "feet" would be then attach parrot to the edge of the pineapple cup.*

8. *Press cloves into the head to make the parrot's "eyes".*

9. *Combine ice cubes, margarita mix as well as 2 cups pineapple chunks in a blender then blend until mostly smooth.*

10. *Pour margarita mixture into pineapple cup, garnish as desired and serve.*

RECIPES

TIP

You can make the parrot up to 3 days ahead of time by wrapping it in a damp paper towel and storing it in a zipper top bag in the refrigerator.

EASY TIC TAC TOE
BREAD

Makes 6-8 servings

Ingredients:

1 round loaf sourdough bread

1/2 cup jarred pesto

Kosher salt and fresh pepper to taste

1/2 cup Parmesan cheese, grated

1 cup mozzarella cheese, shredded

1 bunch green onions

1 bunch basil leaves

Method:

1. Preheat oven to 350°F and line a sheet pan with parchment paper; set aside.

2. Using the SANTOKU KNIFE, slice sourdough loaf at 2-inch intervals, cutting almost to the bottom.

3. Turn loaf around by a quarter turn then cut again as in step 2 to create squares.

4. Using a pastry brush or spoon, spread some pesto over all cut surfaces of the loaf.

5. Season loaf with salt and pepper then sprinkle all over with the cheeses.

6. Transfer loaf to the prepared sheet pan then gather up any spilled cheese and sprinkle on top.

7. Bake for 20-25 minutes or until browned, bubbly and cheese is melted.

8. While loaf is baking, use the 8-BLADE SLICER to create long, pretty strands of green onions.

9. When loaf is done baking, remove and scatter green onions over the loaf.

10. Using the SANTOKU SHEARS, snip basil leaves over the hot loaf before serving.

CUCUMBER
SALAD TWISTS

Makes 4 servings

Ingredients:

2 English cucumbers
2 cups grape tomatoes
1/4 of a small red onion
3 tablespoons apple cider vinegar
2 tablespoons granulated sugar
1 teaspoon kosher salt
1 teaspoon black sesame seeds

Method:

1. *Using the TWIN CURL CUTTER, twist out spirals from the side of the cucumbers to make short spirals (about 7-9 passes through each cucumber, depending on its size).*
2. *Using the SANTOKU KNIFE, cut the tomatoes in half.*
3. *Using the WIDE BLADE PEELER, shave paper thin slices from the onion.*
4. *In a bowl, combine cucumber spirals, tomatoes, onions and remaining ingredients.*
5. *Let stand for 10 minutes stirring occasionally.*
6. *Serve as desired.*

SURPRISE CUPCAKE
BOUQUET

Makes 12 servings

Ingredients:

1 cup unsalted butter, very soft
2 1/3 cups granulated sugar
5 large eggs
3 cups cake flour
3/4 teaspoon baking soda
2 1/4 teaspoons baking powder
2 teaspoons kosher salt
1 cup whole milk
1 cup sour cream
1 tablespoon vanilla extract
1 jar strawberry jam for filling centers
Prepared whipped cream for frosting
A small block of chocolate for shaving
Sprinkles
Ribbon, flower pot and styrofoam ball for the bouquet

Method:

1. *Preheat oven to 350°F and line a cupcake tin with papers; set aside.*
2. *Using a hand mixer, cream butter and sugar for 2 minutes or until fluffy.*
3. *Scrape bowl using a spatula then add eggs and blend them in thoroughly.*
4. *Add in flour, baking soda, baking powder and salt; mix on low speed just until blended.*
5. *Add milk, sour cream and vanilla then mix on low speed until batter is smooth.*
6. *Using the LEVER SCOOP, fill each cupcake well 3/4 full with batter.*
7. *Bake for about 20-25 minutes or until golden brown.*
8. *Remove and let cool completely.*
9. *Using the LARGE CORER, remove center from each cupcake then trim and reserve tops.*
10. *Fill each center almost to the top with jam then replace the trimmed tops.*
11. *Frost tops with whipped cream then use the WIDE BLADE PEELER to shave chocolate over cupcakes before adding sprinkles.*
12. *Tie a ribbon around a flower pot then place a styrofoam ball of similar diameter as the flower pot inside the pot.*
13. *Insert wooden picks halfway into the bottom of the cupcakes then attach to the styrofoam ball to make the "bouquet".*
14. *Serve as desired.*

PINEAPPLE
RICE BOWL

Makes 1-2 servings

Ingredients:

1 pineapple
2 green onions
1 carrot
2 tablespoons canola oil
1 large egg, beaten
Kosher salt and fresh pepper to taste
2 cups rice, cooked
1/4 cup ham, diced
1/4 cup frozen peas, thawed
Soy sauce for serving

Method:

1. *Using the SANTOKU KNIFE, cut the pineapple in half lengthwise from crown to stem.*
2. *Using the SANTOKU KNIFE, cut the core from one pineapple half then use the FRUIT AND VEGETABLE SCOOP to remove the flesh (save other pineapple half for another use).*
3. *Using the CRINKLE CHOPPER, dice pineapple then measure out 1 cup and keep remainder for another use; set aside.*
4. *Using the 8-BLADE SLICER, make long, pretty strands from the green onions; set aside.*
5. *Using the WIDE BLADE PEELER, peel the carrot and use the VEGETABLE CURLER to make long carrot strands then cut strands into 2-inch pieces using the SANTOKU KNIFE; set aside.*
6. *Preheat 1 tablespoon oil in a large skillet over medium-high heat then add the egg; season with salt and pepper.*
7. *Cook egg for 1 minute or until set and brown then flip over and brown the other side.*
8. *Remove egg, chop up using the CRINKLE CHOPPER and set aside.*
9. *Add remaining oil to the pan then add the rice, ham, peas, carrots, green onions and pineapple.*
10. *Add the egg then toss for 2-3 minutes or until hot and steamy.*
11. *Place rice mixture into pineapple boat, garnish as desired and serve with soy sauce.*

TIP
This recipe is great for
using up leftover rice and
vegetables.

CHOCOLATE FONDUE

Makes 4-6 servings

Ingredients:

2 apples
2 kiwi
1 fresh pineapple
8 strawberries

10 marshmallows
Pretzel rods
1 1/2 cups semi-sweet chocolate chips
3/4 cup heavy cream

Method:

1. *Using the TWIN CURL CUTTER, twist out spirals from apples.*
2. *Using the WIDE BLADE PEELER, peel the kiwi then use the CRINKLE CHOPPER to slice them.*
3. *Using the LARGE CORER, punch out cylinders from the pineapple then remove cylinders from the LARGE CORER using the tip of the TWIN CURL CUTTER.*
4. *Using the SANTOKU KNIFE, slice pineapple cylinders into coins.*
5. *Using the 8-BLADE SLICER, make strawberry fans.*
6. *Arrange fruits, marshmallows and pretzel rods on a serving tray.*
7. *Combine chocolate and cream in a microwave-safe bowl.*
8. *Microwave chocolate mixture for 1 1/2 minutes, stir, then microwave for 1 additional minute if needed until melted.*
9. *Pour chocolate into a bowl and place on tray before serving.*

RECIPES

JALAPEÑO POPPERS
WITH CREAM CHEESE

Makes 8 servings

Ingredients:
16 large jalapeño peppers
Kosher salt to taste
1 package (8 ounces) cream cheese, softened
1/3 cup store-bought red pepper jelly

Method:

1. *Preheat oven to 400°F.*
2. *Wearing gloves, use the SMALL CORER to remove the core and seeds of each jalapeño pepper then hollow out or create an open channel with the SMALL CORER and remove the stems if desired.*
3. *Place jalapeño peppers on a parchment-lined sheet pan and season with salt.*
4. *Fill a plastic zipper top bag with cream cheese then snip off one corner.*
5. *Pipe cream cheese mixture into the hollowed out jalapeño peppers.*
6. *Bake for 20-25 minutes or until edges are browned.*
7. *Remove peppers to a serving tray then spoon pepper jelly over peppers before serving.*

WATERMELON
KEG

Makes 1 keg

Ingredients:

1 large watermelon
1 can (12 ounces) frozen cranberry juice concentrate
1 keg spout (see source page 108)
Alcohol such as vodka (optional)

Method:

1. *Using the SANTOKU KNIFE, cut a thin piece from the bottom of the watermelon so that it sits flat (figure 1).*
2. *Using the SANTOKU KNIFE, cut off the watermelon top and set top aside.*
3. *Using the FRUIT AND VEGETABLE SCOOP, remove all the flesh from the watermelon (figure 2).*
4. *Blend watermelon flesh in a blender and strain if necessary then add juice concentrate and refrigerate for a minimum of 4 hours or overnight.*
5. *Using the SMALL CORER, cut a hole into the side of the watermelon for the keg spout (figure 3).*
6. *Adjust hole size using the SANTOKU KNIFE if needed then stick spout into the hole (figure 4).*
7. *Use the pointed end of the TWIN CURL CUTTER to score desired design into side of watermelon.*
8. *Using the SMALL CORER, carve away the green part of the design.*
9. *When ready to serve, pour watermelon punch into the keg and add alcohol if desired.*

TIP

If you accidentally cut the hole for the keg spout too big, you can "glue" it in place using butter. Simply chill the melon to set the butter. The cold punch will keep the butter solid while serving.

MELON BALL
PUNCH

Makes 8 servings

Ingredients:

1 cantaloupe
1 honeydew melon
1 watermelon
2 limes

1 can (11 ounces) frozen lemonade, mostly thawed
2 cups club soda, very cold
3 cups lemon lime soda, very cold
A few mint sprigs

Method:

1. Using the SANTOKU KNIFE, cut each melon in half.
2. Using the FRUIT AND VEGETABLE SCOOP, remove the seeds and strings from the cantaloupe and honeydew.
3. Using the LEVER SCOOP, make balls from all melons (you will have extra melons, keep for another use) then chill melon balls for 2 hours.
4. Using the SANTOKU KNIFE, slice the limes into thin wheels.
5. In a serving pitcher, combine the lemonade and sodas then stir very gently to preserve carbonation.
6. Add melon balls, lime wheels and mint sprigs to the pitcher and stir gently to blend.
7. Serve immediately.

SUMMER FRUIT ROLLS

Makes 6 servings

Ingredients:

1 firm mango
2 kiwi
1 apple
6 sheets rice paper or flour tortillas
12 mint leaves
Zest from 1 lime

For the Strawberry Dip:

1 pint strawberries
1 package (8 ounces) cream cheese, softened
1 cup powdered sugar

Method:

1. *Using the SANTOKU KNIFE, cut off both sides from the mango.*
2. *Using the 8-BLADE SLICER, score mango almost to the peel.*
3. *Using the FRUIT AND VEGETABLE SCOOP, remove mango flesh from peel; set aside.*
4. *Using the SANTOKU KNIFE, trim off both ends from the kiwi then peel using the WIDE BLADE PEELER.*
5. *Using the CRINKLE CHOPPER, slice kiwi into matchsticks; set aside.*
6. *Using the TWIN CURL CUTTER, twist out spirals from the apple; set aside.*
7. *Submerge a sheet of rice paper in hot water for 20 seconds then place on a towel. If using tortillas, simply place one on the counter.*
8. *Take about 1/6th of the mango, kiwi, and apples then place on the bottom third of the rice paper. Top with 2 mint leaves and a small amount of lime zest.*
9. *Roll up like a burrito then place on serving plate. If using tortillas, roll and secure using a wooden pick.*
10. *Repeat to make 5 additional rolls.*
11. *Using the SMALL CORER, hull the strawberries then transfer to a blender or food processor.*
12. *Add cream cheese and sugar to the blender or food processor, blend until smooth then transfer to a serving bowl.*
13. *Cut rolls in half and serve with the strawberry dip.*

DEVILED EGGS

Makes about 16 eggs

Ingredients:

10 large eggs
1/2 cup mayonnaise
2 teaspoons yellow mustard
2 tablespoons sweet pickle relish
1 teaspoon kosher salt
1/2 teaspoon granulated sugar
1/8 teaspoon cayenne pepper
2 teaspoons cider vinegar
1/4 wedge of iceberg lettuce
2 large carrots
2 green onions

Method:

1. *Place eggs into a pot, add enough water to cover by 1-inch then bring to a boil over high heat.*
2. *As soon as water starts to boil, set a timer for 10 minutes and reduce heat to low.*
3. *When time is up, remove pot from heat and add cold water to the pot.*
4. *As soon as you can handle the eggs (while still hot), crack eggs against the side of the pot until cracked all over (so that some water can get between the shell and the eggs).*
5. *Peel each egg under a fairly hard flow of cold water from the faucet.*
6. *Let peeled eggs stand in cold water for about 10 minutes or until completely cool.*
7. *Using the CRINKLE CHOPPER, cut eggs in half lengthwise so that the edges are decorative; save all of the yolks and find another use for any torn egg whites.*
8. *Combine mayonnaise, mustard, relish, salt, sugar, cayenne pepper, vinegar and saved egg yolks in a food processor. Blend until smooth then transfer to a zipper top bag and snip off one corner.*
9. *Pipe yolk mixture into egg white halves.*
10. *Using the SANTOKU KNIFE, shave the iceberg lettuce and place it on serving plate.*
11. *Using the WIDE BLADE PEELER, peel the carrots, use the wavy edge of the VEGETABLE CURLER to score down the length of the carrots then twist carrots through the VEGETABLE CURLER.*
12. *Place carrots and eggs over the lettuce.*
13. *Using the 8-BLADE SLICER, pull pretty strands from the green onions then place strands on each egg before serving.*

STUFFED MINI PEPPERS

Makes 4 servings

Ingredients:

12 mini sweet peppers
8 bacon strips, cooked
1 tablespoon capers
3 pepperoncini peppers
1 can (4 ounces) water chestnuts, drained

2 bunches green onions
1 package (8 ounces) cream cheese, softened
1 cup shredded sharp Cheddar cheese + plus more for topping
Kosher salt and fresh pepper to taste

Method:

1. *Preheat oven to 400°F and line a sheet pan with parchment; set aside.*
2. *Use the SMALL CORER to remove the core and seeds of each pepper then hollow out or create an open channel with the SMALL CORER and remove the stem if desired.*
3. *Place the peppers on the sheet pan.*
4. *Using the SANTOKU KNIFE, chop the bacon, capers, pepperoncini peppers and chestnuts then transfer to a mixing bowl.*
5. *Using the SANTOKU KNIFE, chop 1 bunch of the green onions then add to bowl.*
6. *Using the 8-BLADE SLICER, make long, pretty strands from the other bunch of green onions; set aside.*
7. *Add the cream cheese and Cheddar cheese to bowl, season with salt and pepper then stir until blended.*
8. *Using the LEVER SCOOP, fill each pepper with cream cheese mixture then top with additional Cheddar cheese.*
9. *Bake for 20-25 minutes or until well browned and bubbly.*
10. *Garnish with the green onion strands and serve.*

MEXICAN STREET CORN
SALAD

Makes 4 servings

Ingredients:

6 ears sweet corn
2 avocados
1 small red onion
1 red jalapeño pepper
A handful of cilantro

Zest and juice of 2 limes
2 tablespoons olive oil
1 teaspoon agave nectar or honey
Kosher salt

Method:

1. *Using the CORN ZIPPER, remove all kernels from the cobs over a large mixing bowl.*
2. *Using the SANTOKU KNIFE, cut the avocados in half.*
3. *Using the FRUIT AND VEGETABLE SCOOP, remove the pit and flesh from avocados; discard pit.*
4. *Using the SANTOKU KNIFE, dice the avocado flesh then add to the mixing bowl.*
5. *Using the SANTOKU KNIFE, dice the onion then add to the bowl.*
6. *Using the SMALL CORER, remove the stem, seeds and veins from the jalapeño pepper.*
7. *Using the SANTOKU KNIFE, finely dice the jalapeño pepper then add to the bowl.*
8. *Using the SANTOKU SHEARS, snip cilantro into the bowl.*
9. *Add remaining ingredients to the bowl then stir gently to combine.*
10. *Garnish as desired and serve.*

WATERMELON GOLF BALL

Makes 6-8 servings

Ingredients:

1 mini watermelon or golden Dewlicious melon

Method:

1. *Using the SANTOKU KNIFE, trim the top and bottom off the melon (figure 1).*
2. *Using the WIDE BLADE PEELER, remove all of the peel until white flesh shows (figure 2).*
3. *Using the FRUIT AND VEGETABLE SCOOP, remove large pieces of the melon (figure 3).*
4. *Using the LEVER SCOOP, make balls from melon flesh.*
5. *Using the LEVER SCOOP, create the shallow dimples all over the outside of the melon (figure 4). You can soften the look of the dimple edges by running the WIDE BLADE PEELER over it again if desired.*
6. *Place melon balls inside the melon and serve as desired.*

TURKEY AVOCADO WRAP

Makes 1 serving

Ingredients:

1 large tortilla
2 tablespoons hummus or mayonnaise
A small handful fresh spinach
3 ounces shaved deli turkey
1 small carrot
1 leaf from a head of red cabbage
1 avocado
2 small gherkin pickles

Method:

1. *Place tortilla on a cutting board then spread hummus or mayonnaise on tortilla.*

2. *Add spinach then top with turkey.*

3. *Using the WIDE BLADE PEELER, peel the carrot then peel to make long carrot ribbons.*

4. *Top turkey with carrot ribbons.*

5. *Using the SANTOKU KNIFE, cut red cabbage into thin strips then place over carrots.*

6. *Using the SANTOKU KNIFE, cut avocado in half then use the FRUIT AND VEGETABLE SCOOP to remove the pit and avocado from the skin. Cut into thin slices then place over cabbage.*

7. *Roll up tortilla tightly then cut in half using the CRINKLE CHOPPER or SANTOKU KNIFE.*

8. *Using the 8-BLADE SLICER, make a pretty fan garnish from the pickles and serve.*

ZUCCHINI
PIZZA

Makes 4 servings

Ingredients:

2 large zucchini
Kosher salt and fresh pepper to taste
2 tablespoons Parmesan cheese, grated
1/2 cup pizza or pasta sauce
1/2 cup mozzarella cheese, shredded
1/4 cup mini pepperoni

Method:

1. *Preheat oven to 450°F and line a sheet pan with parchment; set aside.*

2. *Using the SANTOKU KNIFE, cut the ends off of the zucchini then cut in half lengthwise.*

3. *Using the LEVER SCOOP, remove seeds from zucchini.*

4. *Season cut side of zucchini with salt and pepper then scatter Parmesan cheese over zucchini.*

5. *Top each zucchini half with sauce, mozzarella and pepperoni.*

6. *Bake for 25-30 minutes or until brown and bubbly.*

7. *Remove, garnish as desired and serve.*

WATERMELON
MOZZARELLA SALAD

Makes 6 servings

Ingredients:

1 small watermelon
1/2 of a small red onion
Two fresh mozzarella balls (4 ounces each)
A few fresh basil leaves
A few fresh mint leaves
Kosher salt and fresh pepper to taste
3 tablespoons extra virgin olive oil
2 tablespoons red wine vinegar

Method:

1. *Using the SANTOKU KNIFE, cut the watermelon in half.*
2. *Using the FRUIT AND VEGETABLE SCOOP, remove large chunks of watermelon then use the LEVER SCOOP to make balls from flesh.*
3. *Using the WIDE BLADE PEELER, shave the onion into thin strands.*
4. *Using the CRINKLE CHOPPER or SANTOKU KNIFE, dice up the mozzarella cheese.*
5. *Using the SANTOKU SHEARS, snip the basil and mint leaves.*
6. *Combine all ingredients in a mixing bowl, toss gently and serve immediately.*

TROPICAL SORBET IN
PINEAPPLE BOATS

Makes 4-6 servings

Ingredients:

1 ripe pineapple
1/2 cup granulated sugar
1 red apple
1 green apple
Assorted tropical-flavored sorbets
A few mint sprigs

Method:

1. *Using the SANTOKU KNIFE, cut pineapple in half including the green fronds at the top.*
2. *Using the FRUIT AND VEGETABLE SCOOP, remove the flesh, avoiding the pineapple's core.*
3. *Using the SANTOKU SHEARS, snip out the core then use the FRUIT AND VEGETABLE SCOOP again until the pineapple's inside is clean.*
4. *Place empty pineapple halves on a sheet pan and freeze until needed.*
5. *Using the CRINKLE CHOPPER, finely chop the pineapple flesh then transfer to a microwave-safe bowl.*
6. *Add sugar to the bowl, stir to combine then microwave for 4-6 minutes or until boiling.*
7. *Remove and keep hot.*
8. *Using the TWIN CURL CUTTER, twist out spirals from the apples; set aside.*
9. *When ready to serve, dip the LEVER SCOOP into a cup of hot water, scoop sorbets into the frozen pineapple boats, garnish with apple spirals and mint then serve with the hot pineapple sauce.*

WACKY WATERMELON CAKE

Makes 1 cake

Ingredients:

1 large watermelon
1 small watermelon
1/2 of a cantaloupe
1/2 of a honeydew
2 pints fresh blueberries
Cake wires (see source page 108)

Method:

1. *Using the SANTOKU KNIFE, cut the large watermelon in half then turn over onto flat side and cut off rind, shaping it into a rough drum shape (figure 1).*

2. *Using the SANTOKU KNIFE or FRUIT AND VEGETABLE SCOOP, make the sides and edges round then cut a slice from the top using the SANTOKU KNIFE to cut it at an angle (figure 2). Set aside unused melon portion for later use or discard.*

3. *Repeat steps 1 and 2 with other large watermelon half, trimming this middle "cake" tier to a smaller diameter than the base tier.*

4. *Repeat steps 1 and 2 with the small watermelon for the top "cake" tier. You now have a large, medium and small tier (use SANTOKU KNIFE to trim as needed).*

5. *Stack the tiers on a cake pedestal using wooden picks to secure (figure 3).*

6. *Using the FRUIT AND VEGETABLE SCOOP, remove the seeds and strings from the cantaloupe and honeydew.*

7. *Using the LEVER SCOOP, make honeydew balls then use the WIDE BLADE PEELER to make ribbons from some of the honeydew and the cantaloupe.*

8. *Place blueberries around the top tier and on cake wire ends.*

9. *Place a honeydew ball on the top tier then stick the cake wires into it.*

10. *Arrange a row of thin honeydew balls around the middle tier.*

11. *Roll up honeydew and cantaloupe ribbons then coil up into flowers and place around the bottom tier (figure 4).*

12. *Serve as desired.*

TIP

As an alternative method, you can use the WIDE BLADE PEELER to make the rough drum shape smooth after step 1.

103

DIY NOODLE BOWL

Makes 1 serving

Ingredients:

Handful of snow peas
1 small carrot
1 garlic clove
1 fresh ginger coin
1 green onion
1 small bundle dry mung bean or rice noodles
1 teaspoon bottled sriracha chili sauce or to taste
Handful of leftover chicken, ham, shrimp or tofu
1 tablespoon soy sauce or to taste
1/2 teaspoon sesame oil
2 cups boiling water

Method:

1. *Place the snow peas into a canning jar or other transportable container.*
2. *Using the WIDE BLADE PEELER, peel the carrot.*
3. *Using the VEGETABLE CURLER, create thin carrot ruffles from carrot then place over snow peas.*
4. *Using the SANTOKU KNIFE, mince the garlic and ginger then place over carrots.*
5. *Using the 8-BLADE SLICER, make long strands from the green onion then place half of the strands in the jar.*
6. *Layer noodles, sriracha, chicken, soy sauce, oil and remaining green onions over jar contents.*
7. *Store jar in the refrigerator for up to 2 days if desired.*
8. *When ready to serve, add 2 cups boiling water to jar, cover and let stand for 3 minutes to heat jar contents and soften the noodles then stir to combine.*
9. *Garnish as desired and serve.*

TIP

This is a great recipe to use up leftover meat, vegetables, grains and pasta.

PINEAPPLE FRUIT DIP

Makes 8 servings

Ingredients:

1 ripe pineapple

2 packages (8 ounces each) cream cheese, softened

1/4 cup toasted coconut + more for the top

1/2 cup granulated sugar

2 kiwi

1 pint basket strawberries

2 cups large marshmallows

Handful of pretzel rods

Method:

1. Using the SANTOKU KNIFE, cut off a little piece from the pineapple bottom so that it sits flat.
2. Using the SANTOKU KNIFE, cut pineapple in half horizontally. Use one pineapple half for this recipe and keep the other half for another use.
3. Using the FRUIT AND VEGETABLE SCOOP, remove the pineapple flesh going around the core.
4. Using the SANTOKU SHEARS, snip out the core.
5. Using the LARGE CORER, carve a scalloped edge around the pineapple.
6. Measure 1 1/2 cups of the smaller pineapple scraps then place in a blender.
7. Using the CRINKLE CHOPPER, slice remaining pineapple flesh and place on a serving platter.
8. Add the cream cheese, coconut and sugar to the blender then blend until smooth.
9. Pour pineapple mixture into hollowed out pineapple.
10. Using the WIDE BLADE PEELER, peel the kiwi then use the CRINKLE CHOPPER to cut into slices.
11. Place remaining items around pineapple dip, garnish with additional toasted coconut and serve.

TWISTED BREAD & BUTTER PICKLES

Makes 4 servings

Ingredients:

2 English cucumbers
1/4 cup apple cider vinegar
2 teaspoons kosher salt
2 tablespoons granulated sugar
2 teaspoons pickling spice

Method:

1. *Using the TWIN CURL CUTTER, twist out spirals from the side of the cucumbers then transfer to a mixing bowl.*
2. *Add remaining ingredients to the bowl then toss to coat.*
3. *Refrigerate for 1 hour then serve as desired.*
4. *Store in an airtight container in the refrigerator for up to 1 week.*

SOURCE PAGE

Here are some of my favorite places to find ingredients that are not readily available at grocery stores as well as kitchen tools and supplies that help you become a better cook.

Chocosphere
P.O. Box 2237
Tualatin, OR 97062
877-992-4623

Excellent quality cocoa (Callebaut)
All Chocolates, Jimmies and sprinkles
www.chocosphere.com

D & G Occasions
625 Herndon Ave.
Orlando, FL 32803
407-894-4458

My favorite butter vanilla extract by Magic Line, cake and candy making supplies, citric acid, pure fruit oils, professional food colorings, ultra thin flexible spatulas, large selection of sprinkles and jimmies, unusual birthday candles, pure vanilla extract, pastry bags and tips, parchment, off-set spatulas, oven and candy thermometers, kitchen timers
www.dandgoccasions.com

Penzeys Spices
P.O. Box 924
Brookfield, WI 53045
800-741-7787

Spices, extracts, seasonings and more
www.penzeys.com

The Bakers Catalogue at King Arthur Flour
135 Route 5 South
P.O. Box 1010
Norwich, VT 05055

Pure fruit oils, citric acid, silicone spatulas, digital timers, oven thermometers, real truffle oil, off-set spatulas, measuring cups and spoons, knives, ice cream scoops, cheesecloth, microplane graters, cookie sheets, baking pans
www.kingarthurflour.com

Fortune Products, Inc.
205 Hickory Creek Road
Marble Falls, TX 78654
830-693-6111

Hand-held Accusharp knife sharpeners
www.accusharp.com

Rolling Pin Kitchen Emporium
P.O. Box 21798
Long Beach, CA 90801
949-221-9399

Cheesecloth, inexpensive "harp" shaped vegetable peelers, measuring cups and spoons, knives, vast array of kitchen tools including microplane graters, blow torches, baking pans and dishes
www.rollingpin.com

Nui Enterprises
Vanilla from Tahiti
501 Chapala St. Suite A
Santa Barbara, CA 93101
805-965-5153
www.vanillafromtahiti.com

Whole Foods
550 Bowie St.
Austin, TX 78703
512-477-4455

Grains, citric acid, natural and organic products, xanthan gum, gluten-free baking items, real truffle oil, miso paste
www.wholefoods.com

Gluten Free Mall
4927 Sonoma HWY Suite C1
Santa Rosa, CA 95409
707-509-4528

All ingredients needed for gluten-free baking
www.glutenfreemall.com

Amazon.com
Keg spouts and Duff Goldman cake wires
www.amazon.com

INDEX

FOR ALL OF MARIAN GETZ'S
COOKBOOKS AS WELL AS
COOKWARE, APPLIANCES, CUTLERY
AND KITCHEN ACCESSORIES
BY WOLFGANG PUCK

PLEASE VISIT
HSN.COM
(KEYWORD: WOLFGANG PUCK)